All human beings originally made in the image and likeness of God intuitively know that there is a God and search for Him instinctively. The human soul is lonely and cannot find fulfillment in the treasures of this world. Only the ultimate experience of finding God and achieving a right relationship with Him brings satisfaction. The birthright of all God's children is to be born again into His family and to worship Him. Our hope of glory is to see Him and be like Him.

"And ye shall seek me, and find me, when ye shall search for me with all your heart" (Jeremiah 29:13).

God's Answers to the Mystery of Life

Albert C. McCann

A BARBOUR BOOK

Scripture quotations in this volume are from the King James Version of the Bible.

ISBN 1-55748-394-9 Cloth
ISBN 1-55748-360-4 Paper

© 1990 by Albert C. McCann
Published by Barbour and Company, Inc.
Box 719
Uhrichsville, OH 44683
Printed in the United States of America

Contents

Foreword

To know the author is to know a man who is totally committed to the veracity of the Bible.

I have been privileged to know Al McCann for over fourteen years. He came to the Village Church after retiring from an executive position with the Ford Motor Company.

I soon recognized him as a gifted teacher and writer. When it comes to the inerrancy of the Scriptures, he is uncompromising. He is a true student and a man of the Book. His writings witness to his spirituality, and his insight shows a practical relationship to the Christian life.

William B. Bedford, D.D.
Pastor Emeritus
Christian and Missionary Alliance Church
Shell Point Village, Florida

Preface

I dedicate this book to the glory of God. My goal is to magnify Jesus Christ in language that the reader will enjoy, to explain the necessity and the miracle of the new birth as simply and concisely as I can, and to make God's holy will and His scriptural exhortations to grow to our full potential comprehensible to all the saints.

The multiplicity of Christian denominations, church traditions, and differing doctrines are often confusing to those seeking truth. The growth of the cults, the liberal compromises of many professing Christians, and the holier-than-thou attitude of some of the dearest saints are hurting the work of the Lord's church. The excuse for these divisions—that we all interpret Scripture differently—is unacceptable to me. I submit that our problems are due entirely to a lack of prayerful reading of the Bible and our schisms are the result of disobedience to its clear teachings.

It is my belief that today's church needs a revival of Bible reading. The Bible is the Word of Truth, and we are not to be led by human philosophy, by our emotions, or by the "way that seemeth right unto a man," but by the written Word of God. The Bible alone is infallible, and when the Holy Spirit is allowed to be our teacher, the truth of the Word will make us free.

These articles were written to provide biblical answers to specific questions that often come up during Bible study. Often Christians are left unsatisfied by the prepared lessons in their Sunday school quarterlies. Often they are disappointed by the opinions of the most renown theologians and their endless books. Christians need to know what God has said about these matters.

The poems included here are original. Sometimes our most sincere and joyful thoughts are best expressed by old-fashioned poetry.

My sons, Roger and Mark, and their families have been a source of inspiration and encouragement to me. Their children are my final endowment and blessing.

My wife, Marge, has been my dearest companion and friend. Her loving patience as she typed and retyped this manuscript has been my greatest help. Her faith in me and her support through all my years of teaching will never be forgotten.

1
The Mystery of Life

*And as we have borne the image of the earthy, we shall also
bear the image of the heavenly.*

1 Corinthians 15:49

Life is a mystery: Science can determine neither its origin nor
its ultimate destination. We know that it inhabits certain kinds of
substances for a while, then it departs and the substance turns to
dust.

The current search for life on other planets intrigues us. We
wonder if, in all the starry host of heaven, life is to be found only on
this one infinitesimal speck of dust we call earth. Also, if life is only
a product of chance, as some insist, why are there so many forms of
life and varying degrees of intelligence concentrated in the peculiar
atmosphere of a single planet?

Satisfactory answers to all our questions about life are found
only in Scripture. If, as the Bible tells us, the heavens were made to
declare the reality and the glory of an eternal Creator to a lost but
intelligent creation, then it all begins to make sense.

Any scientifically honest consideration of the mystery of life, the
beauty and order of the universe, and the wonder of our adventure
must conclude that there is a cause, an intelligence, and a power
only the God of the Bible can fulfill. To say that it all occurred by
chance and ends without purpose is a ludicrous philosophy. Life was
created for a magnificent and eternal purpose, as we shall soon see.

2
Ode to the Mystery

What is life?
Is it nothing more than an accidental mixture
Of certain chemicals on one remote planet?
If so, it has no purpose.

We have learned
That nothing occurs without a cause.
Substance cannot create itself from nothingness,
And who conceived life's various identities and
Degrees of intellect?
What are we striving for?
We must all die, regardless of attainments.
If death is final, why are we so short-lived
In an ageless universe?

I submit that there is more!
We are the creation of an Almighty Intelligence,
Who is preparing an eternal masterpiece.
This life is not the end.

What is sin?
There appears to be an attempt to spoil the creation
By an evil, spiritual influence,
And he is succeeding in the lives of many.

Where shall we look
For the answers to all these things?
Is there not a supernatural Book
From an omnipotent One?

3
The Bible

All scripture is given by inspiration of God, and is profitable for doctrine, for reproof, for correction, for instruction in righteousness: That the man of God may be perfect; thoroughly furnished unto all good works.

2 Timothy 3:16, 17

The Bible is the Christian's most precious earthly possession. God speaks to us from the Bible, and apart from the Word, we cannot know the way of salvation or God's holy will for our lives.

So many today are trying to earn their way to heaven by doing good works. The Bible says they are deceiving themselves. The way of salvation is a gift; it cannot be earned. Jesus said, "I am the way, the truth, and the life: no man cometh unto the Father, but by me" (John 14:6). The Bible, God's written Word, reveals Christ, the living Word, as the only way we may be saved.

After we are saved, we are only babes in Christ. We need to feed on the Word, that we may grow thereby (*see* 1 Peter 2:2). If we neglect the Word, we cannot be workmen in the Lord's church. We must prayerfully read and meditate on God's Word to grow to our full potential. Those who never become rooted and grounded in the Word are the most likely to fall away or to succumb to false teaching. The psalmist has rightly said, "Thy word have I hid in mine heart, that I might not sin against thee" (Psalms 119:11).

The Bible is a source of comfort beyond compare. In every trial of life, we find help, hope, and the strength to carry on in the pages of this blessed Book.

Finally, the Bible contains the answers to the *Mystery of Life.* We need to remember that God is the Bible's author; men wrote it under the instruction of the Holy Spirit. Our Lord Jesus Christ, by His life, death, and resurrection, confirmed the truth of the Scriptures. He was literally the Word made flesh and the fulfillment of

Scripture. The Holy Bible is the only infallible source of truth in all the physical universe!

4

Being Born Again

Except a man be born again, he cannot see the kingdom of God.

John 3:3

Why is there so much confusion over the new birth? I believe it is because Satan blinds the eyes of all who search outside the written Word of God. He deludes mankind not by denying the truth of Scripture, but by encouraging us to search elsewhere.

So we look to human teachers, human philosophy, and man-made religions. We contemplate ways "which seemeth right unto a man, but the end thereof are the ways of death" (Proverbs 14:12). It seems right that we should do good works, but the Bible says we cannot earn salvation. It seems right that we should be baptized and join a local church, but the Bible says we must do these things after we are saved. It seems right to believe in Jesus Christ, and we cannot help but assent to the proven, historical truths regarding Him, but the Bible says, "the devils also believe, and tremble" (James 2:19).

Then what must we do to be saved from eternal death and be born again? The Apostle John wrote, "But as many as received him [Jesus Christ], to them gave he power to become the sons of God, even to them that believe on his name: Which were born, not of blood, nor of the will of the flesh, nor of the will of man, but of God" (John 1:12, 13). Scripture declares that when the Holy Spirit speaks to us through the written or spoken truth of the Word of God, we become convicted of our own sinfulness and our need to repent and be saved. At that moment, the Savior is knocking at our heart's door, and all we must do is *receive* Him! When we do this, we are born again into the family and household of God.

Salvation is the gift of God to all who believe and act on this simple biblical truth: When we accept God's unspeakable gift, the Holy Spirit revives our dead spiritual nature and we are spiritually reborn. The acceptance of Jesus Christ is a supernatural, wonderful, and unforgettable experience—unlike anything that has ever happened to us before—and we who have experienced it are never the same again. We are new creations who desire, above all else, to do the will of God, because He is now our Father!

Taste and See

"Give us a sign of His glory,
Show us the Father," they cried,
"Can we believe such a story?"
They asked when the Savior died.

"Who is this King," they flouted,
"Submitting to nail and prod?"
"Come down from the cross," they shouted,
"If thou art the Son of God!"

As far as the world could see then,
He died with the darkened sun,
And only to those who believed Him
Returned the arisen One.

Only to those who knew Him
Came power and joy and love,
More power than those who slew Him,
More knowledge of things above.

Men still are too busy to bother,
To learn of the crucified One.
They'd ask for no sign of the Father,
If only they knew the Son.

Seeking a way of life complete,
They doubt, and their doubts defeat them.
You can't prove oranges are sweet
To men who will not eat them.

5
Baptism

He that believeth and is baptized shall be saved.

Mark 16:16

The word *baptize* comes from the Greek *baptizo,* which means to consecrate by covering with water. It was initiated by John the Baptist and, as administered by him, was a baptism of repentance. We know that John baptized in the river Jordan and, apparently, his converts waded in for the ceremony. We are not told exactly how it was done. We do not know whether John totally immersed them or poured water over their heads. Certainly it was more than just a sprinkling. You wouldn't need to wade into a river to be sprinkled! I personally believe that total immersion best typifies being buried with Christ in the likeness of His death. "Therefore we are buried with him by baptism into death" (Romans 6:4).

But again, nowhere in the New Testament are we told exactly how the ceremony was to be performed. Therefore we have no right to be dogmatic about our opinion.

When Jesus came to be baptized by John, John was aghast. "I have need to be baptized of thee," he said, "and comest thou to me?" (Matthew 3:14). And the Lord answered, "Suffer it to be so now: for thus it becometh us to fulfil all righteousness" (Matthew 3:15). When Jesus said "us," He was identifying Himself with sinful mankind. Though He was sinless, yet He knew that soon He must become sin for us (*see* 2 Corinthians 5:21) and suffer for our sins so that we might be made righteous.

John's baptism was primarily for God's chosen nation (the Jews), calling them to repentance. When the apostles of our Lord began baptizing, they baptized in the name of the Lord Jesus. That was a baptism of consecration. As Jesus identified Himself with sinners in His baptism, so we identify ourselves with Him in the Lord's baptism.

Baptism is not optional. All of the Lord's converts were baptized. Though Jesus, Himself, did not baptize, His apostles did (*see*John 4:1, 2). After our Lord returned to heaven, the apostles taught that all believers were to be baptized. "Then Peter said unto them, Repent, and be baptized every one of you in the name of Jesus Christ for the remission of sins, and ye shall receive the gift of the Holy Ghost . . . Then they that gladly received his word were baptized" (Acts 2:38, 41).

Later, the Gentile believers were included: "Can any man forbid water, that these [Gentiles] should not be baptized, which have received the Holy Ghost as well as we? And he commanded them to be baptized in the name of the Lord" (Acts 10:47, 48).

It is noteworthy that the Gentiles received the Holy Ghost before they were baptized, as a sign to the Jews, and Peter then commanded them to be baptized into the body of Christ.

It is also significant that only genuine believers (disciples) were baptized. Nowhere in the Scriptures is it recorded that infants were baptized. The final command of our Lord was to make disciples and then baptize them. "Go ye therefore, and teach all nations, baptizing them in the name of the Father, and of the Son, and of the Holy Ghost. Teaching them to observe all things whatsoever I have commanded you" (Matthew 28:19, 20).

Finally, I believe it is not the mode of baptism that is important, but the sincere desire of the believer to be obedient to the Lord's clear commands. I believe that submitting to the ordinance of baptism is the Christian's first step in a life of obedience to God. It is also a public demonstration of our unashamed desire to be identified with Him.

6
Who Are the Saints?

Paul and Timotheus, the servants of Jesus Christ, to all the saints in Christ Jesus which are at Philippi, with the bishops and deacons.

Philippians 1:1

It is noteworthy that the apostles of our Lord wrote to the saints, distributed for the necessity of the saints, and prayed for the saints. The saints referred to in Scripture are all the redeemed of mankind, both living and dead. They are saved sinners, and none are considered any more holy than the others. In fact, they are admonished to "let each esteem other better than themselves" (Philippians 2:3).

Nowhere in Scripture is any church or church overseer given authority to declare sainthood upon anyone; certainly not upon the dead. The New Testament clearly teaches that all who have accepted Jesus Christ as Savior and Lord are saints. More than that, we are also priests, every one of us. "But ye are a chosen generation, a royal priesthood, an holy nation, a peculiar people" (1 Peter 2:9).

As believer-priests, we have direct access to God. We need no other mediator besides our Lord Jesus Christ. We are admonished to "confess your faults one to another, and pray one for another, that ye may be healed" (James 5:16).

The saints are the joy of the Lord, kept by the power of His blood. He will never forsake them; "they are preserved for ever" (Psalms 37:28). Isn't that wonderful?

7

The Set of the Soul

sh

What manner of man is this, that even the winds and the sea obey him!

Matthew 8:27

I love the sea, and I have always admired those who know how to sail. It must provide a feeling of great accomplishment to feel and master the silent strength of the wind, to sail with it, to turn about and tack against it.

In my only sailing experience, I was entrusted by friends to tend the spinnaker in their small boat. We were in a race on the Detroit River, and we led all the way while the wind was behind us! I never knew the skill involved in taking down a billowing spinnaker, turning about, and facing the wind. Due to my clumsy efforts, we came in last.

Life is like that: It's great when we're sailing with the wind, but there are times when we cannot avoid adverse or stormy winds. How wonderful it is then to know that we have a Father in heaven who watches over us, understands our human frailties, and will help us if we ask.

The course of our lives is not determined by fate or by circumstances. The storms that God allows are for our own good, designed to make us able seamen and to help us grow to our fullest potential.

God has a plan for every life, a particular course for each of us to follow. We can win the race if we are willing to set our souls to know and do His holy will.

Like ships at sea, we travel
The storm-tossed journey of life.
It's the set of the soul
That determines the goal,
And not the calm or the strife.

8

A Father's Wish

A father wishes his son to be
A greater, wiser man than he.
So very early he has a plan
To make the boy a superman.

He holds those newborn fingers long,
To demonstrate that they are strong,
And startles all with shouts of glee
At baby's too-fat anatomy.

And later when to his dismay,
There are no muscles to display,
He reasons that he can expect
The kid's a super intellect.

So what, if he can't throw a ball?
What this world needs most, after all,
Is genius, and a father's pride
With such success is satisfied.

But then on Parent-Teacher day,
He sees some schoolwork on display,
And though he laughed off "Show and Tell,"
The kid can neither write nor spell!

This brings about in every case
That long-avoided face-to-face,
"Let's talk it over, son, and see
What kind of man you're apt to be.

"There must be something you enjoy,"
The father tells his restless boy.

And soon he learns there is, alright,
It's girls, the car, and Saturday night!

A father wishes his son to be
A greater, wiser man than he.
But good fathers learn as the years do flee,
The importance of prayer and humility.

Greatness is more than human acclaim,
Wisdom is more than scholastic fame,
And life is not worth living until
We've learned our *heavenly* Father's will.

God, too, has a wish for every life,
And every human care and strife
Is allowed for a purpose known above
As we walk in the watch-care of His love.

How thankful then a father can be
When his wish is granted so differently,
For greater the bond between father and son
As together they live for the glorified One.

9
Living for Jesus

I am crucified with Christ: nevertheless I live; yet not I, but Christ liveth in me: and the life which I now live in the flesh I live by the faith of the Son of God, who loved me, and gave himself for me.

Galatians 2:20

Living for Jesus is no easy task. The above Scripture from the heart of the Apostle Paul refers not only to our position in Christ, but also to our daily walk. Positionally, and mysteriously, we are crucified with Christ because of who we are. When we accepted Him as our Savior, He forgave all our sins: past, present, and future. He took up residence within us, and we are a new creation in Him. We were obediently baptized into the likeness of His death and raised from the waters of baptism in the likeness of His resurrection, all by God's grace.

It is not difficult to be crucified with Christ positionally, because He did all the work. He endured the suffering for your sins and mine. But the apostle was also thinking of the cost of living for Jesus. He was thinking of self-crucifixion!

The primary objective of the Christian life is to bring glory to His name, which we do by our daily walk in obedience to His holy will. This isn't easy, because Satan will buffet the obedient Christian. He is not concerned with the disobedient; they are no problem.

Obedience to God's will requires the filling and leading of the Holy Spirit, and most of us don't know *how* to be filled. One thing I do know: It doesn't happen through occasional emotional experiences during a church service. *The Holy Spirit fills prepared and dedicated temples only!* If we want to be filled with the Spirit so that only God is glorified by the good works that we do, we must, first of all, crucify the sins of the flesh that hinder the work of the Spirit. As long as we are yet in Adam's likeness—until we are physically translated (glorified) into the image and likeness of Christ—we will need to do battle with the sins of the flesh.

When we were first saved, we quickly put to death the more obvious sins. With God's help it was not hard to quit cursing, telling dirty jokes, carousing, and so forth. It is not hard to put on the Christian veneer. We start going to church regularly, and we do good works. However, there are millions of "good" people who aren't saved, who go to church regularly, and who do good works. So what makes us different?

"And they that are Christ's have crucified the flesh with the affections and lusts" (Galatians 5:24).

Have we? If we are honest, we must admit that we still have problems with the sins of the flesh. So many Christians spoil their testimony by their fits of temper, by their pride, by their selfishness, by their covetousness, and by all the sins that so easily beset us. We are generally not willing to crucify these sins as God has commanded us, and consequently we have no power at all with God.

"For the flesh lusteth against the Spirit, and the Spirit against the flesh: and these are contrary the one to the other: so that ye cannot do the things that ye would" (Galatians 5:17).

The Christian who really wants to obediently live to the glory of God will be tested by the works of the flesh. Satan wants to destroy our testimony, and he knows our weaknesses, even though our brothers and sisters in the church may not.

"Now the works of the flesh are manifest, which are these; Adultery, fornication, uncleanness, lasciviousness, Idolatry, witchcraft, hatred, variance, emulations, wrath, strife, seditions, heresies, Envyings, murders, drunkenness, revellings, and such like" (Galatians 5:19-21).

If you wonder about the "such like," you should know these verses:

These six things doth the Lord hate: yea, seven are an abomination unto him: A proud look, a lying tongue, and hands that shed innocent blood. An heart that deviseth wicked imaginations, feet that be swift in running to mischief, A false witness that speaketh lies, and he that soweth discord among brethren.

Proverbs 6:16-19

We could go on and on, naming different sins. The truth is, the Holy Spirit brings conviction to the hearts of true believers regarding the particular sins that are hindering their personal testimony. When we are convicted, we can do one of two things: We can harden our hearts and quench the Spirit, or we can repent. By repenting, we put to death that particular sin. We can do that because the power of God is at our disposal, and "greater is he that is in you, than he that is in the world" (1 John 4:4).

Other convictions will follow, and as we continue to crucify our sins of the flesh, God will bless us and we will grow spiritually into the kind of prepared vessel the Holy Spirit of God can completely fill and use. Gradually the fruit of the Holy Spirit will become more and more manifest in our daily lives. As Jesus said, "Wherefore by their fruits ye shall know them" (Matthew 7:20). We cannot bring forth both good fruit and bad fruit and still glorify our Father in heaven. Brethren, it is not so much what we don't do, but what we do that the world really notices. The world needs to see the fruit of the Holy Spirit in our daily lives. _That is how God is glorified!_

"But the fruit of the Spirit is love, joy, peace, longsuffering, gentleness, goodness, faith, Meekness, temperance: against such there is no law" (Galatians 5:22, 23).

These characteristics of Christ do not suddenly appear as an instantaneous gift when we are saved, nor do they come as some miraculous "second blessing." _They are hard earned!_ The fruit of the Spirit is seen most in mature believers who are willing to sacrifice themselves and all their earthly possessions, if necessary, for the cause of Christ. Christians who are filled with the Spirit are those willing to crucify the flesh so that their works will bring glory to God.

Jesus said, "Let your light so shine before men, that they may see your good works, and glorify your Father which is in heaven" (Matthew 5:16).

It isn't easy, but it will be worth it all. We have God's Word on that.

Our Gifts

He gave of his substance ungrudgingly,
And he passed not a stricken man by,
"For my kindness shall be
My redemption," said he,

But his deeds weren't recorded on high.

She sang of the Savior so gloriously
That she thought, as the song left her throat,
How the church would be filled
With a music that thrilled,
And the Risen One heard not a note.

He prayed with a fervor that filled every eye
Of those in attendance with tears,
But his praise was so loud,
That the love he avowed
Never reached to those heavenly ears.

"By grace are ye saved; through faith," said the Lord,
Not of works lest we boast and be vain,
Let's humbly surrender
Each talent we tender,
That the glory to God may remain.

10
Prayer

And this is the confidence that we have in him, that, if we ask anything according to his will, he heareth us.

1 John 5:14

The act of prayer is the Christian's most precious privilege. The Lord's disciples were quick to note that when Jesus drew apart from them for private prayer, He always returned encouraged, refreshed, and strengthened. So very early in our Lord's earthly ministry, the disciples came to Him and said, "Lord, teach us to pray." The Lord then taught them the model prayer that we have all learned and love. He taught them the importance of secret prayer, to specifically ask for things in His name, and above all, to pray that God's will might be done.

Likewise the Spirit also helpeth our infirmities: for we know not what we should pray for as we ought: but the Spirit itself maketh intercession for us with groanings which cannot be uttered. And he that searcheth the hearts knoweth what is the mind of the Spirit, because he maketh intercession for the saints according to the will of God.

Romans 8:26, 27

What a *mysterious* but wonderful promise! When we are not sure what we should pray for, God's Holy Spirit prays for us so God's will might be done. Our sincere desire to know and do the will of God is much more important than our words. We are instructed to pray believing that God always answers our prayers, but sometimes God says, "No." Sometimes He says, "Wait." Sometimes He says, "I have a better plan for you." We don't always get exactly what we ask for, but when we ask according to His will, we have the confidence that we will receive what is best. God knows our needs better than we do.

Finally, we should recognize that real prayer is communication and fellowship with our Father in heaven. Prayer involves listening and meditating on His Word. By reading the Bible prayerfully, we give God a chance to speak to us, and such two-way conversation provides us with understanding, blessing, and comfort that can be found in no other way.

Like the disciples, we should learn to pray very early in our Christian experience, for prayer is the secret of successful living!

Prayer is the secret of the Christian's success.
When we kneel, Almighty God's attention is claimed;
Though brief our prayer, or when we all our sins confess,
Our heavenly Father's ears are yet constrained.

Prayer is a source of strength beyond compare.
When we kneel, our Father's will to seek anew,
The omnipotence of God is ours to share
In completion of the task He bids us do.

Prayer is fellowship: sweet, joyful, filled with love.
When we kneel, heaven's angels gather 'round,
And Christ is at the Father's side above,
And He in us and we in Him are found.

Prayer is mysterious, beyond our finite way.
When we kneel, God's Holy Spirit intercedes
With groaning we neither hear nor seek to say,
For He alone knows all our earthly needs.

Prayer is fearful, though too often we forget.
When we kneel, Satan trembles, for he knows
He must somehow intervene or else regret
Each moment that we spend in such repose.

Prayer is the breath of humans born again.
When we kneel, our spirits are renewed and fed.
We rise a little taller, wiser, kinder men.
We rise to walk where Christ's dear feet have led.

11

God's Sure Word

In the beginning was the Word, and the Word was with God, and the Word was God.

The philosopher Plato echoed the plea of all humanity when he cried, "Oh that God might send forth a word!" Mankind needs the assurance that God is, that He cares, and that He will somehow reach down and save us.

God has answered that plea. I submit to you the Gospel record as the Apostle John has penned it: "In the beginning was the Word, and the Word was with God, and the Word was God. . . . And the Word was made flesh, and dwelt among us, (and we beheld his glory, the glory as of the only begotten of the Father), full of grace and truth" (John 1:1, 14).

Brethren, God has given mankind a sure Word. What more could He have done? In what greater way could He have shown His love and given us undeniable proof of His existence?

First, He promised through His written Word that He would send into the world a Savior. He gave us the time and the place and the exact conditions under which the prophecies would be fulfilled. Jesus Christ was born, He lived, He died, and He rose again in fulfillment of God's sure Word. Also, He came in human form, so man might see God through Him. He spoke the plan of salvation with human lips, and He paid with His life for human sins. Finally, He rose from the grave as He promised, proving that He was indeed the Son of God, proving beyond all doubt the truth of the ancient Scriptures.

He could have come in power and great glory, with all His holy angels, but such an appearance would not have brought us salvation. That would not have been a revelation of His love, but of His glory, His majesty, and His power! All the world would have feared and worshiped such an appearance, but not one soul would have been saved from death and hell.

God doesn't want our worship to be born of fear. God is love. He wants us to love Him as He loves us. "Perfect love casteth out fear: because fear hath torment. He that feareth is not made perfect in love" (1 John 4:18). God has planned a future existence for those who truly love Him, one in which there will be no more fear, sin, or death. Jesus said, "that whosoever believeth in him should not perish, but have everlasting life" (John 3:16).

The Apostle Peter, speaking of the truth of the written Word of God, points to Jesus as the fulfillment of the Old Testament prophecies. "We have also a more sure word of prophecy; whereunto ye do well that ye take heed, as unto a light that shineth in a dark place, until the day dawn, and the day star arise in your hearts" (2 Peter 1:19). Jesus Christ is God's sure Word. He is "the way, the truth, and the life" (John 14:6). God sent Him forth to meet man's every need. He is the *unspeakable gift* of Christmas!

The First Christmas

He came with no glittering crown on His brow,
Befitting the Maker of heaven and earth.
The angels commanded no knee to bow
At His humble birth.

Not as the conqueror comes to the throne
O'er the pathway his legions have wrought,
He came as a tender babe to His own,
And they knew Him not.

Seeking our love, not our fear of His wrath,
He bled for our sins and was slain,
That we, who believe He was God, through faith
Shall with Him reign.

12

The Wise Men

Now when Jesus was born in Bethlehem of Judaea in the days of Herod the king, behold, there came wise men from the east to Jerusalem, Saying, Where is he that is born King of the Jews? for we have seen his star in the east, and are come to worship him.

Matthew 2:1, 2

Not much is really known of the wise men, except that they came from an Eastern land, possibly Persia. We don't know how many there were, and certainly the scriptural account does not describe them as kings or stargazers. The term *wise men* means that they were more learned than their contemporaries. It undoubtedly is meant to convey that they had knowledge of the ancient writings. They were more likely scribes or priests than kings. Apparently they had read at least some of the Hebrew Scriptures, for they knew that the One to be born was to be king of Israel, that His sign would be a star, and that He was worthy of their worship! This in itself is amazing, considering the stature of Judaea, a small remnant of the once-mighty nation of Israel that was now only a ragtag tribe under the heel of Rome.

It is apparent and significant that only these wise men saw His star that shone first in the East that holiest of nights when our Savior was born. I believe that from their studies they knew the time was at hand, and they were looking for His star.

"I shall see him, but not now: I shall behold him, but not nigh: there shall come a Star out of Jacob, and a Sceptre shall rise out of Israel" (Numbers 24:17).

There is no mention in the Bible of the shepherds being guided by a star. The sign given to them by the angels was that they would find "the babe wrapped in swaddling clothes, lying in a manger" (Luke 2:12). I imagine they scurried through the town knocking on many doors before they found the Christ child.

Certainly, there was no star to guide the soldiers of Herod!

The star was *not* a conjunction of two of the planets in our own solar system, as some of our modern teachers are explaining. Had this been so, all the region of the Mideast would have seen it. Furthermore, there is no way a conjunction of planets could have led the wise men to a particular house in Bethlehem.

It was a miracle star! It was His star! It appeared to the wise men first on the night of our Lord's birth. It led them on a journey of several months to Jerusalem, then it disappeared. After their encounter with Herod, it miraculously reappeared and led them to Bethlehem, "till it came and stood over where the young child was" (Matthew 2:9). No ordinary star or conjunction of planets could do that!

"And when they were come into the house, they saw the young child with Mary his mother, and fell down, and worshipped him" (Matthew 2:11). Apparently, by the time the wise men arrived, Joseph had found a house for Mary and the young child while he completed his business in Bethlehem.

Brethren, I believe our Lord's star never drew a crowd because it was intended only for those wise men who looked for it and had faith enough to believe in it. How sad that Israel slept through it all!

Jesus said of Himself, "I am the root and the offspring of David, and the bright and morning star" (Revelation 22:16). Every time I gaze at the morning star, I wonder, "Will this be the day of His coming?" Will we see Him first in the distance as a bright star? One thing I do know—Only those who "love his appearing" will see Him! "And unto them that look for him shall he appear the second time without sin unto salvation" (Hebrews 9:28).

I submit that the wise men of the twentieth century are neither the stargazers, nor the kings, nor the philosophers of this world, but those who know and believe the promises of the Holy Scriptures and are looking for His star. I believe the rest of the world will sleep on, as Israel did, while we who are watching are caught up to meet Him in the air!

Christmas Night

O beautiful night, spread thy cloak on the earth,
Shine, O lamps of the heavens, again,
For upon such a night did a virgin give birth

To a babe and a king of all men.
O beacon of light far away in the east,
Guide me now as the wise men were led.
For the joy that I seek, the hopes and the peace,
I can see in the light far ahead.

How needless and faithless to ask for a sign,
For the glow of His love I discern,
And sure as the stars of the heavens will shine,
I am sure of my Savior's return.

13

New Year's Resolutions

I can do all things through Christ which strengtheneth me.
Philippians 4:13

Whatever happened to the practice of making New Year's resolutions? Even if we didn't always keep them, they were worth the effort; any resolve to do better is good. We all have faults that need correcting: We could all be more thoughtful and considerate of others, we all need to grow spiritually and become more mature Christians.

Why not resolve this year to make better use of our God-given talents? God's Holy Spirit is the giver of special gifts, and every child of God is a recipient. "But the manifestation of the Spirit is given to every man to profit withal" (1 Corinthians 12:7). There is at least one thing each of us can do that no one else can do—or no one else can do quite as well. *There is no excuse for mediocre Christians;* we ought to be the best at whatever we do!

Our final destiny is heaven, but our earthly fate and our reward in heaven depend on what we do here—what we accomplish for God and our fellowman depends on our own initiative. God will help us to move mountains, if necessary, but they won't budge if we don't even try! Let's not be fatalists. Let's make our lives shine for God's glory. As the Apostle Paul has written, "I can do all things through Christ which strengtheneth me" (Philippians 4:13).

Man's Destiny

What forces 'round us plan our paths ahead?
Are we drawn by unseen strings and then,
That day we are pronounced to be quite dead,
Cut loose in some deep abyss of forgotten men?

Does destiny really bind each newborn soul
Against its will and lead it to some goal
Prepared upon an altar we call fate,
Its consequences realized too late?

Are we a people, or puppets on display,
With no purpose of our own to gain,
Nor able to rebel and truly say,
"This life is mine to live and make remain."
If so, our destinies are planned,
How useless then for man to lift a hand.
For better or for worse, his state remains
The same as fate has said, despite his pains.

I won't believe there's nothing we can do!
My fate is not determined by the stars.
God has a plan for everyone, it's true,
But the choices that we make are only ours.
We can God's Holy Word ignore
And choose to seek what earth may have in store;
Or we can seek through His own holy light
The way of truth, of confidence, and might.

There is a Savior who has passed this way
And promised man need never walk alone.
He shares the joys and sorrows of each day.
He listens to each child He calls His own.
Our hopes and plans He helps us to achieve.
Though mountains interfere, if we believe,
The goals we seek are won, and God in love
Has plans for greater victories above!

14
Heaven

I go and prepare a place for you.

I really get excited when I think about heaven! Before He left us, Jesus told His disciples, "I go and prepare a place for you" (John 14:3). They were then privileged to see Him rise up into heaven in bodily form, "and a cloud received him out of their sight" (Acts 1:9). After that, the disciples went on their way rejoicing and proclaimed the good news with boldness. After that, they knew that heaven is not just a spirit world, a condition or state of awareness after death. They knew that heaven is a real place!

Three different heavens are described in the Scriptures. The first is the lower heaven, or the region of the clouds. The second is planetary heaven, the region of the stars, so vast that finite man can never see or travel beyond them. The third heaven is the abode of God. The blessed hope of the Christian church is that someday we shall be transported to our Father's house, where, with an escort of holy angels, we shall see God face-to-face!

This earth is beautiful. I love the sea and sky, the forests and the mountains, all the living things that God has created here. But did you ever stop to think that it has all been spoiled by the evil influence of Satan and our sins? We are living on a condemned planet. Everything that this earth has to offer is only temporary; none of us know how much longer we shall dwell here.

God has planned something far better for those who love Him. Jesus promises those who believe in Him that He will come again "and receive you unto myself; that where I am, there ye may be also" (John 14:3). The third heaven will be more wonderful than we can even imagine!

Heaven

Though enthralled by earthly beauty,
I find my eyes are much inclined
To search beyond their normal duty,
Beyond the scope of finite mind.
Somewhere I perceive a planet
A million years from care and strife.
In my dreams, I easily span it
To a more abundant life.

Irrespective of the pundit,
I'm resolved to satisfy
My own desire, to aspire
Above a sphere condemned to die,
To perfection in the sky.

15
The Trinity

But there is a spirit in man: and the inspiration of the Almighty giveth them understanding.

Job 32:8

One of the *mysteries* of God most difficult for the finite mind to comprehend is the Holy Trinity. God the Father; God the Son; and God the Holy Spirit are three—and yet they are only One. The word *Trinity* appears nowhere in the Bible, yet it is inescapably declared there. It is spoken of so naturally that we see it as more than doctrine. The Trinity of God and God's creation is the essence of reality!

First, the Scriptures reveal God the Father as the unseen source, the power and cause of all things. Secondly, we see God the Son, who tangibly and visibly reveals the Father to mankind as He perfectly executes the will of God on earth. Then we find ourselves administered to by God the Holy Spirit, who is unseen and yet reveals God through redeemed mankind and the written Word of God by His inspiration. All three are equally One, equally eternal, and equally God.

Now consider the physical universe, which logically should reflect its Creator. All knowable things in the universe may be classified under the headings of space, matter, and time—a trinity!

Space consists of three dimensions. There would be no space, no reality, if there were only two dimensions. Space is cubical. To ascertain the contents of a cube, we do not add the length, the width, and the height; we multiply them. The mathematics of the Trinity is not one plus one plus one, but one times one times one, which equals one to the third power! Brethren, it is not by chance that the holy city described in the Book of Revelation is equal in length and width and height. It is our eternal home!

Matter involves these three distinct parts and no other. Each involves the whole of matter, and none of the three can exist alone.

First there is energy, the cause. Second there is motion, which reveals and is begotten by energy. Third there are phenomena, which proceed from motion and reveal the whole of matter. Just as the Holy Spirit reveals the Son, and through Him, the Father, to mankind!

The third item in the physical universe is time. Time is one entity, but it is in turn a perfect trinity consisting of the past, the present, and the future. These are three-in-one from the viewpoint of our eternal God, who, not bound by the dimensions of time, is the great I AM!

Finally, let's look at the trinity of God's ultimate masterpiece—mankind. The Word of God tells us that we are composed of a body, a soul, and a spirit. Originally made in the image and likeness of God, we also are a trinity. It has always been helpful to me, in considering the functions of the body, the soul, and the spirit, to examine the three types of life God has created.

Our bodies, for example, apart from our soul and spirit, are similar to plant life. Plants are living bodies, sensitive to their surroundings. They are born, they grow, they reproduce, and they return to the dust of the earth. However, they have no consciousness of life.

Animals are the second form of life God created. Animals, in addition to being sensitive to their surroundings, have an awareness of life. They experience feelings such as pain, fear, anger, joy, and contentment. Animals are self-conscious. They have a soul, for the soul is the awareness of life.

But man is more. God breathed into his nostrils and added a *third* element—the spirit. It is the spirit in man that makes him like God. It is the spirit that makes all mankind God-conscious. No animal has this same awareness. The spirit in man came from God, and like God, it is eternal. When an animal dies, his soul, or the awareness of life, dies with his body. When a man dies, the soul is still fully conscious. This is because that third element of spirit, embodied in the soul, continues to keep that soul alive. The spirit came from God, and so it must return to God and give account!

"But there is a spirit in man: and the inspiration of the Almighty giveth them understanding" (Job 32:8).

"And the very God of peace sanctify you wholly; and I pray God your whole spirit and soul and body be preserved blameless unto the coming of our Lord Jesus Christ" (1 Thessalonians 5:23).

Let us not doubt the reality of the Holy Trinity of God, for it is reflected in all His creation. And though our present bodies, marred by sin, must return to the dust of the earth, our eternal souls will soon be clothed in new and glorified bodies so that we will be like Him forever!

16
The Grandeur of the Firmament

I thrilled as I gazed at the stars last night,
Many millions of light-years high,
And I studied their merry twinkling light
As it danced in the velvet sky.

Oh, their majesty seemed to frighten me,
For I felt so suddenly small,
And I thought of the Lord watching tenderly
O'er the magnitude of it all.

The heavens were clear and the wind was still,
And the glorious scene left me awed,
Till I longed to climb to the steepest hill,
That I might be nearer to God.

17
Wisdom

If any of you lack wisdom, let him ask of God.

James 1:5

Any normally intelligent human being can acquire knowledge. We can soak it up in school, from books, from practical experience, and by prudent observation and listening throughout our lives. The human brain has unlimited capacity to store up knowledge, but such a filling does not necessarily make us wise! The Word of God tells us that, "The fear of the Lord is the beginning of knowledge: but fools despise wisdom and instruction" (Proverbs 1:7).

I believe a wise man will seek first of all a right relationship with his Creator. Otherwise, the accumulation of knowledge is vain self-glorification. It has no eternal profit and, "As for man, his days are as grass: as a flower of the field, so he flourisheth. For the wind passeth over it, and it is gone; and the place thereof shall know it no more" (Psalms 103:15, 16).

Wisdom is a gift from God. We all have it, but we so often fail to recognize where it came from and how to use it. Wisdom is recognition of our purpose for living and the need of an ultimate objective with eternity's values in mind.

The wicked are not wise; they are blinded by vanity, insensitive to the pleadings of the Holy Spirit of God. They seek knowledge to gain worldly fame and treasures that rot or are stolen. "Unto you, O men, I call; and my voice is to the sons of man. O ye simple, understand wisdom: and, ye fools, be ye of an understanding heart" (Proverbs 8:4, 5).

A wise man will recognize that God exists and has an interest in the affairs of men. A wise man will turn to the Word of God for knowledge. He will seek to know the will of God and will learn the need for salvation from sin and eternal hell. A wise man will accept the unspeakable gift of God and make Jesus Christ his Savior and Lord. Then, with such a sure foundation to build on, he will desire more and more knowledge. He will enrich his own life and the lives he touches as he learns what it means to live to the glory of God! Then he will learn the purpose for his life and the eternal objectives his heavenly Father has planned.

"Then shalt thou understand the fear of the Lord, and find the knowledge of God. For the Lord giveth wisdom: out of his mouth cometh knowledge and understanding" (Proverbs 2:5, 6).

There is no excuse for a foolish Christian. We need to be knowledgeable. However, we also need to be spiritually wise, so the good we do be not "evil spoken of" (*see* Romans 14:16). *We must never forget who we are and Whom we represent.* We need not fail, for the wisdom of God is available to the sons of God, if we only ask! "If any of you lack wisdom, let him ask of God, that giveth to all men liberally, and upbraideth not; and it shall be given him" (James 1:5).

Three Questions

If a mighty oak in the forest
Came crashing to the ground,
Were there no ear
Nearby to hear,
Would there be any sound?

When the golden sunset settles
O'er the brink of an azure sea,
Were there no eye
To view the sky,
Would there any color be?

When the warmth of the summer winds
Do blow after winter's storm,
Were there no hand
To touch the land,
Would it blossom cold or warm?

Such earthly knowledge God ordains
His presence to reveal
No purpose can

It serve but man,
To let him hear, and see, and feel.

And when His handiwork we view,
Our finite minds ascent
To mansions where
He plans to share
A glory earth can't comprehend.

18
Charisma

But by the grace of God I am what I am: and his grace which
was bestowed upon me was not in vain.

1 Corinthians 15:10

Modern theologians have added the word *charismatic* to their
growing list of labels for believers with varying points of view:
fundamentalists, evangelicals, neo-orthodox, and so forth. The
charismatics ostensibly are those who "feel the Spirit" more than
others. Actually, the term is only another confusing, unnecessary
misnomer.

All who have been born again into the family of God are temples
of the Spirit of God. Our subsequent spiritual growth is directly
proportional to our yieldedness to the teaching and leading of the
Spirit. However, the Holy Spirit can teach us nothing if we neglect
a prayerful study of the written Word of God. Without the Word,
we will remain carnal and are apt to be led by the spirit of error. All
our variances are attributable to our not "rightly dividing the word
of truth" (2 Timothy 2:15).

Brethren, our faith must not be based on feelings and emotions,
but wholly on the finished work of Jesus Christ and the infallible
Word of God. We are saved by grace and nothing more. We know
that we are possessors of the Holy Spirit primarily because the Word
of God tells us so. We experience the fruits of the Spirit when we
are obediently yielded. Special gifts of the Spirit are given as God
determines. Again, it is all of God's grace.

The word *grace* is actually derived from the Greek *charis,* so in
the real biblical sense, only Christians who daily appropriate divine
grace can have genuine charisma. All other charisma is earthly and
of no eternal value.

God's grace is not a one-time gift; His matchless grace is a past,
present, and future experience. Grace not only wrought our salva-

47

tion, but is poured out on the believer day after day. "And of his fulness have all we received, and grace for grace" (John 1:16).

Thus the appropriation of grace is not just a "second blessing," but there is one grace after another and spiritual blessing upon spiritual blessing until our cup runneth over!

Charisma emanates from the Father. It is made obtainable through the Son, and it is *supernatually* applied to yielded, obedient, and humble believers by the operation of the Holy Spirit.

19

The Word

In the hustle and bustle of life every day,
Engulfed in the clamor and lost in the sway
Of human endeavor, it's easy to stray
From the Word.

Mid the crashing crescendo of life on a sphere,
That is tuned to the clashing of pinion and gear,
No mention of Christ and His love do we hear,
Not a word.

Through trials and testings mankind is obsessed,
Striving for things only briefly possessed,
Forgetting that treasures in heaven are blest
In the Word.

Till eventide reckons that labors should cease,
Till loved ones and home bring us joy and release,
And we look in God's Book for rest and the peace
Of the Word.

20
Christian Stewardship

And the Lord said, Who then is that faithful and wise steward,
whom his lord shall make ruler over his household.

Luke 12:42

What is meant by Christian stewardship? According to Webster, "A steward is one who superintends the affairs or possessions of another." For example: If I owned a stable of thoroughbred horses and I hired someone to take charge of those horses—someone to make certain they were properly housed, exercised, fed, and groomed—that person would be my steward. If my horses were not properly cared for, if they were neglected in any way, I, as owner, would hold the steward responsible and accountable. A steward is responsible for the possessions entrusted to him by another.

As a Christian, I am a steward of all that God has entrusted me to possess. None of my possessions really belong to me. They belong to God, but He has made me steward over them.

What are some of these things? First of all, He has given me life itself. He has given me certain talents. He gives me the air I breathe, the food I eat, and the strength for each day. He gave me a wonderful Christian mother, a lovely wife, and two sons. He gave me an earthly home. He gave the life of His only begotten Son on Calvary's cross for me. He has given me new life through faith in His Son, instilled His Holy Spirit within me, and given me His Holy Word, the Bible, to guide me through this life.

He can take away from me any one or all of these things at any time! All that I have belongs to Him, but in His infinite mercy and grace, He allows me to call them all my own.

Christian stewardship is not giving, as some have implied, for I have nothing to give. God has already taken back my mother. He could also take my wife, my boys, my health, my home, and all that I have whenever He chooses. They are all part of His plan for me, blessings entrusted to me because God loves me. But as a steward, He is holding me responsible and accountable for them all.

God has given me a free hand. I can use the life He has given me for His glory, or I can serve the devil. I can profitably redeem the time He has given me, or I can waste it. I can use my money for good things or for evil. I can instruct my children in the way of the Lord or I can let them learn the ways of the world. I can allow the Spirit of God to fill me and use me, or I can ignore Him. I can read and obey the Word of God, or I can choose to do that which seems right in my own eyes.

But I am certain that someday I must face God and give account for the way I have managed His affairs and His possessions!

Christians are called to be good stewards of the time, talents, and possessions God has entrusted to their care, but this is not all! Christian stewardship is even more.

You and I, as Christians in an unbelieving world, are stewards of the greatest and holiest possession of all! Were we not empowered by the Holy Spirit, such a stewardship would be unthinkable. *I'm talking about the matchless grace of God.*

"As every man hath received the gift, even so minister the same one to another, as good stewards of the manifold grace of God" (1 Peter 4:10).

We hear much about the love of God, and we acknowledge His marvelous grace, but do we realize that we are the stewards of that grace? If that marvelous, matchless grace we sing about is not seen in our homes, in our schools, in our communities, and in our nation—if it is not being shed abroad—it is because we Christians are unfaithful stewards.

It is not *our* love, but God's love, that this sick old world needs today. And we who call ourselves Christians are the only means that God has to make His love manifest. If God's grace is not seen in us, it will not be seen at all. It is not enough for me to pray for my fellowman; I must tell him of the love of God and then show him by my helping hands how much God really cares! This is Christian stewardship.

Jesus said to His disciples, "He that believeth on me, the works that I do shall he do also; and greater works than these shall he do" (John 14:12).

God has empowered us by His Spirit to do His holy will. We are the visible manifestation of Christ, His lips, His hands, and His feet. We are the body of Christ and members in particular.

This is what the Apostle Paul meant when he wrote, "For to me to live is Christ" (Philippians 1:21). This is what Christian stewardship is all about.

21
Dream of the Rapture

Last night I dreamed
The starlight through my window
Was calling me,
Some mystery to foretell.
A heavenly light
Was shining on my pillow,
A heavenly light
Across my eyelids fell.

Last night I heard
A trumpet call from heaven,
In notes more sweet
Than any earthly tone.
The music filled
My room with sounds of heaven,
The music thrilled
My heart with joy unknown.

Then in the sky,
Bright angels were descending.
I watched with awe
Their faces as they passed.
My longing eyes
Sought whom they were attending.
I longed to rise
To see the Lord at last.

I had no fears,
But then I thought of others,
And there were tears
For lost ones close beside.
I could not wait

To plead again, my brothers.
It was too late
To bring you to His side!

Last night I dreamed
The heaven burst asunder,
And evermore
I'll tell the Gospel true,
How God will come
For those who watch with wonder,
To take us home,
To realms forever new.

22

Christian Joy

Enter thou into the joy of thy lord.

Matthew 25:21

Christians have more joy than any other of God's creatures. What greater joy can the human heart experience than the realization that the Creator of the universe has personally chosen, called, redeemed, and claimed us for His own?

We might have doubts about our being chosen by God, if not for the fact that God lets *us* decide. Jesus said, "for many be called, but few chosen" (Matthew 20:16). These words have mystified the world's most renowned theologians, but the child of God understands. God is omniscient: He knows the past, the present, and the future. He knew from the foundation of the world who would accept His Son as Savior, and He chose them for eternal glory.

When we, by our own free will, accept Jesus as our Savior, we are "born again" into the family of God. We become brothers and sisters in Christ; we are related by the same precious blood. We find a "peace that passeth all understanding"(*see* Philippians 4:7). Our joy is made full in living for Jesus Christ as His personal ambassadors. Our citizenship is in heaven, but even in this life we enjoy a sweet fellowship that this world knows little of.

We have trials, but only those that our heavenly Father allows. They are meant for our good. They make us wise, humble, compassionate, and mature, and so we accept them with thanksgiving.

23

The Christian's Hope

A Risen, Living, Coming Lord

Some said the other day,
"I think you need explain
The happiness your eyes display,
The peace of heart you claim.
Tough trials sore have come your way,
You never do complain.

"When all around you, others frown
And grumble at the night,
Because the rain is coming down,
And things aren't going right,
You sing as though you wore a crown!
What makes your life so bright?"

I replied, "Deep down inside,
My hope is made secure
That life eternal doth abide
Beyond this transient door.
The Word made flesh can't be denied,
He lives forevermore!

"I know He lives and reigns above.
He reigns within my soul,
I'm ever conscious of His love,
His will is all my goal,
And things I should be fearful of
Are under His control.

"My life is filled with joy and peace.
Through trials I can sing;

And when this life shall someday cease,
I know that heaven will bring
From earthly confines, God's release
To realms where anthems ring!"

24
God the Holy Spirit

God is a Spirit: and they that worship him must worship him in spirit and in truth.

John 4:24

When we are born again into the family of God through faith in Jesus Christ, we find true answers to all the problems of mankind, for we become possessors of a right relationship with God the Father. We become children of God, and this is an everlasting relationship. *However, the challenge of living for Jesus as His witnesses requires a right relationship with God the Holy Spirit.* This is a relationship not fully achieved by all God's children, and its absence is the reason we lack power.

When we are born again, we are born of God the Holy Spirit. We become new creatures. Our new life is a miracle of God, just as much a miracle as the birth of Jesus by the virgin Mary, for we were both fathered by the same Holy Spirit.

Being born of the Spirit, we are also indwelt by the Spirit. When we say we have Jesus Christ in our hearts, we should recognize that He dwells there in His Spirit. Jesus promised, "And I will pray the Father, and he shall give you another Comforter, that he may abide with you for ever" (1 Corinthians 6:19). The Apostle Paul wrote, "What? know ye not that your body is the temple of the Holy Ghost which is in you?" (John 14:16). In Romans 8:9, the apostle also wrote, "Now if any man have not the Spirit of Christ, he is none of his." Brethren, *all who are saved of God are possessors of God the Holy Spirit.* Our problem is that we refuse to let Him completely possess us!

We don't have to do any work to be saved: Salvation is the gift of God, and all we must do is accept it. When we accept salvation, we accept Jesus as our Savior, but it is up to us to make Him our Lord! This means submitting ourselves to the direction of God the Holy Spirit. It requires feeding on the Word of God for spiritual growth (*see* 1 Peter 2:2). It requires self-denial. The Apostle Paul so admonishes us in Romans 12:1, "I beseech you therefore, brethren, by the mercies of God, that ye present your bodies a living sacrifice, holy, acceptable unto God, which is your reasonable service."

A right relationship with God the Holy Spirit requires that we keep His temple clean, holy, and available for His use. It requires obedience. Even as Joshua, in leading the children of Israel into service for God in Canaan, said, "Sanctify yourselves: for to morrow the Lord will do wonders among you" (Joshua 3:5). When we are born again, we are sanctified by God for eternal glory, but we must *sanctify ourselves for service!* Someone has wisely said that God does not always use the most capable, but He uses the most available. God fills the clean and prepared and willing believer with His Holy Spirit, and uses him for His glory.

25

God Is There

What a blessing it is to know Him:
To commune with Him daily in prayer,
To know He is near when you need Him,
To feel His presence there.
What gladness to know He is watching,
Our joys and our sorrows to share.
What a comfort to know
That wherever we go,
He is there, He is always there.

What a thrill to be going to heaven,
What a Light to assure us the way,
What a wonderful promise He's given
Of His returning someday.
What mansions are waiting in glory,
In a world He has gone to prepare.
How we long to arise
To our home in the skies,
He is there, He is always there.

26

The Invitation

For I think that God hath set forth us the apostles last, as it were appointed to death: for we are made a spectacle unto the world, and to angels, and to men.

1 Corinthians 4:9

There are those who say it is old-fashioned and unnecessarily melodramatic when a minister of the Gospel gives an invitation for folks to come forward and publicly confess Jesus Christ as Savior and Lord of their lives. "You don't have to do that to be saved, do you?" Of course not. You can be saved right where you sit, or at home and alone with God. "Then why walk down the aisle of the church?" they ask. "Why make a spectacle of yourself?"

Perhaps we should look to the Scriptures regarding this matter. First: How are we saved? The Bible says:

That if thou shalt confess with thy mouth the Lord Jesus, and shalt believe in thine heart that God hath raised him from the dead, thou shalt be saved. For with the heart man believeth unto righteousness; and with the mouth confession is made unto salvation. For the scripture saith, Whosoever believeth on him shall not be ashamed.

Romans 10:9-11

Brethren, if we really believe in Jesus, we cannot help but confess Him before others! We don't have to walk down the aisle of a church, but somehow we must make our first confession. We must take that first step of our new walk, and if we can't even walk down the aisle of a church where other Christians are praying for us, how will we ever confess Him in the hostile atmosphere of the world? When the pastor says, "Come," it is the Evil One who says, "Don't do it. Don't make a spectacle of yourself."

I am reminded of Joshua, one of the great Old Testament heroes who fearlessly spoke up for the God of Abraham, Isaac, and Jacob and again and again proclaimed his faith in the promises of God in the face of disbelief, fear, and scorn on the part of his contemporaries. In his last days he counseled and charged Israel with these words: "choose you this day whom ye will serve; whether the gods which your fathers served that were on the other side of the flood, or the gods of the Amorites, in whose land ye dwell: but as for me and my house, we will serve the Lord" (Joshua 24:15).

I wonder how many men today can speak like that for themselves and their houses? The proclamation of the Gospel is a God-given responsibility for all Christians, but the primary responsibility is given to men as heads of their households. I think it is significant that our Lord chose twelve *men* to be His apostles. So many men I know seem ashamed to speak of Jesus. Are we so intellectual that we are ashamed of the childlike simplicity of the real Gospel? If not, then we need to stand up like men and be counted for the Lord! We are commanded to confess Him before others, and when men in the home and men in the church do this, revival comes.

It is true that walking down the aisle of a church doesn't save you, but it can help you. It may give Satan his first real defeat in your life! It is a meaningful public confession of your inward faith. It is only a first step, but it is also a first victory, and it will strengthen you for the road ahead.

I'll tell you something else it will do: It will bring you a fullness of joy you have never known. I've never heard anyone say he was sorry he took that first step. However, there are so many who are sorry, and whose hearts are hardened to the pleading of God's Holy Spirit, because they kept putting it off!

Finally, our public confession brings joy to other Christians. I know it always brings tears of joy to my eyes when someone makes his or her first confession of Christ. And when a *man* walks down the aisle, I feel like shouting, "Hallelujah!" For there goes a whole household. It almost always works that way.

When we confess our Savior publicly, it makes our salvation experience real, joyful, and a blessing to others. It prepares the way for a lifetime of witnessing in His holy name and for His sake. *I think that even the angels in heaven sing out when we make spectacles of ourselves for Jesus.*

27

My Faith

About my faith, I hesitate
To tell, for I confess
I have no triumphs to relate.
No mountains have I moved, unless
I can with humble candor state
The Lord is my success.

My Savior is my only pride,
He gives me joy divine.
Though rough my path, He's been my guide,
He makes His peace be mine.
His love for me can't be denied,
He's ever by my side.

My faith no trial can erase,
Nor doubts subvert my vows,
I know the troubles I must face
Are those which He allows.
My grief is tempered by His grace,
My losses He endows.

It all has purpose. Don't you see?
God has a Master Plan,
And preparing me for eternity
He willed since time began.
He gave His only Son for me
That I might live again.

I cannot therefore be downcast.
My faith, though not so great as some,
Assures me when this life is past,
The best is yet to come.

I'll see my Savior's face at last,
As angels take me home!

28

The Theory of Evolution

So God created man in his own image, in the image of God
created he him; male and female created he them.

Genesis 1:27

Under modern scientific scrutiny, the theory of evolution is falling apart at the seams. Most of the original evidence for evolution has been disproved, and what's left is on highly doubtful ground. The Neanderthal man, for example, now appears to be a product of race degeneration rather than of a developing race. Recent discovery of human remains predating both Neanderthal and Cro-Magnon skeletons are spectacular in revealing earliest man as gigantic in size, walking fully erect, and having huge brain cavities that indicate a race of super men with super intellects.

The Bible tells us that plants and animals can only bring forth after their own kind. New genetic research has proven that chromosome changes, gene mutations, and hybridization can produce new varieties or species, but all the evidence thus far in the genetic field proves conclusively that these changes cannot go beyond certain narrow limits and certainly cannot produce new *kinds* of life.

God's declaration of a finished creation absolutely refutes the theory of continual evolutionary creation. True science confirms the Scriptures.

The basic principle of all physical science is that of the conservation and deterioration of energy. The law of conservation of energy states that in any transformation of energy in a closed system, the total amount of energy remains unchanged. The law of conservation of mass states that although matter may be changed in size, state, or shape, the total mass cannot be changed. In other words, this first law of thermodynamics teaches us that no creation or destruction of energy or matter is taking place in the physical universe.

The second law of thermodynamics enunciates the corollary law of energy deterioration. In any energy transformation, although the total amount of energy remains unchanged, the availability of that energy decreases. In any closed mechanical system, as long as any energy change is taking place, some of the energy is being lost to nonrecoverable friction or heat energy. This is why it is impossible to build a perpetual-motion machine.

This same principle applies to the physical universe. Practically all the earth's energy comes from the sun. However, the greater part of that tremendous energy is dissipated in space in the form of unrecoverable heat. Eventually the sun must burn itself out, and when it does, all activity on earth will cease. This applies to all the stars of the universe; they are all running down and growing old.

A universe that is growing old must have had a definite beginning! In short, this law of energy deterioration affirms the truth of creation and the existence of the Great Creator.

But shame on us, if we have to wait for science to disprove the various theories that are at variance with the Word of God. Christians should not accept as truth anything that contradicts the Bible. The Bible alone is infallible! *It reveals God's Answers to the Mystery of Life.*

Of old hast thou laid the foundation of the earth: and the heavens are the work of thy hands. They shall perish, but thou shalt endure: yea, all of them shall wax old like a garment; as a vesture shalt thou change them, and they shall be changed: But thou art the same, and thy years shall have no end.

Psalms 102:25-27

29
What Is Man?

When I consider thy heavens, the work of thy fingers, the moon and the stars, which thou hast ordained; What is man, that thou art mindful of him?

Psalms 8:3, 4

Many of the world's most renowned scientists, astronomers, and astronauts have undoubtedly asked the same question when they view and consider the magnificence and scope of the universe. It is so vast that the finite mind cannot comprehend it! Our entire solar system is but a speck in the galaxy of stars in which we dwell, and we know that our galaxy, the Milky Way, is only one of a countless universe of star galaxies in the heavens. Outer space is endless.

This boggles the mind. Our comprehension of things eternal is subject to the limitations of our sinful human flesh. We can no more understand the heavens than we can understand our eternal God, except to know that they declare His glory (*see* Psalms 19:1). But God has promised all who truly believe and trust in Him that we shall someday see Him *and be like Him! (See* 1 John 3:2). Then we will witness the creation of new heavens and a new earth that will be ours to know, understand, and inhabit forever!

The Bible tells us that man was created in the image and likeness of God (*see* Genesis 1:26, 27). The first man did not crawl out of the sea or have to learn to walk erect. He was created out of the earth, and immediately upon his creation, he looked exactly as God had intended. Adam and Eve were perfect humans with perfect minds and bodies. If they had not sinned, they would have lived forever.

When God the Father, God the Son, and God the Holy Spirit said, "Let us make man in our image, after our likeness," (Genesis 1:26), man was created a trinity consisting of a spirit, a soul, and a body, yet being only one, even as God is One. However, when Adam sinned, he died spiritually that very day (*see* Genesis 2:17). He also began to die physically. He no longer possessed eternal life. He could no longer live in the Garden of God or partake of the tree of life. He had to return to the dust from which he came.

Such is the condition of every descendant of Adam. We are born in the image and likeness of sinful Adam (*see* Genesis 5:1-3). We are born spiritually dead! That is why Jesus said, "That which is born of the flesh is flesh; and that which is born of the Spirit is spirit. Marvel not that I said unto thee, Ye must be born again" (John 3:6, 7).

When we are born again, we are born of the Holy Spirit of God. His Spirit revives our own dead spirits so we are once again the triune beings that God intended. We are made whole (*see* 1 Thessalonians 5:23). As new creatures, we are changed from the likeness of Adam and grow spiritually into the likeness of our Lord, yet not completely, for though our souls are saved, we must continue in these sin-ruined bodies until the resurrection. Adam's likeness must be returned to the dust, as God has said.

In the resurrection we shall become all that God has planned from the foundation of the world. We shall be more glorious than the angels; we shall be like Him! That is the purpose for which we were created. We are God's family, His pearl of great price. We will inherit a brand-new universe that shall never know sin. Man is God's greatest creation, and that is why God is mindful of him.

30
A Father's Prayer

Train up a child in the way he should go: and when he is old,
he will not depart from it.

Proverbs 22:6

Modern psychologists maintain that a child's most formative years are from birth to age three, when his personality and character are most moldable. After that, we parents all resort to various motivative, promissory, and desperate disciplinary measures! Finally in their teen years, we establish and try to enforce our own "Because I said so," authoritative, mandate-type, house rules! Most often, in utter frustration we bemoan the well-publicized generation gap.

But should we expect our children to be perfect? We are not yet the mature parents that God wants us to be. As a Christian parent, I think the following verses of Holy Scripture apply to both parents and children: "Not as though I had already attained, either were already perfect: but I follow after . . . I press toward the mark for the prize of the high calling of God in Christ Jesus" (Philippians 3: 12, 14).

Our Father in heaven understands our human weaknesses, and even as adults, we continue to grow in the hands of the Master Potter. Christian parents who have tried to bring up their children in the nurture and admonition of the Lord know their work is never really done. Even though our children are grown and have children of their own, their mother and I continue to pray for them.

So, Mom and Dad will do their best,
And look to God to do the rest.
We recognize mistakes we've made,
Our own great weaknesses displayed
In each of these two boys we've raised.

But we have faith, our Lord be praised,
Where we have failed, God will make
His image grow for Jesus' sake!

31

What Is Woman?

*And the rib, which the Lord God had taken from man, made
he a woman, and brought her unto the man. And Adam said,
This is now bone of my bones, and flesh of my flesh: she shall
be called Woman, because she was taken out of Man.*

Genesis 2:22, 23

Eve was created to be a helper, a suitable companion for Adam
(*see* Genesis 2:18). The animals could not fill this role, for they were
not equal spiritual beings with whom the man could have a Godfearing fellowship. The first woman came from the body of the first
man. She was part of his bone and flesh. Genesis 2:22, 23 utterly
refutes the theory of evolution. You cannot even believe in theistic
evolution unless you deny the Holy Scriptures!

The words of Adam apply to every married woman as much as
they applied to Eve, for the Scriptures say, "Therefore shall a man
leave his father and his mother, and shall cleave unto his wife: and
they shall be one flesh" (Genesis 2:24). A woman's primary purpose
in life is, of course, to serve God, but if she marries, she is intended
to be a suitable companion to her husband. More than this, she is
to submit to his headship, "For the husband is the head of the wife,
even as Christ is the head of the church" (Ephesians 5:23).

Every married woman has the same relationship to her husband
as the church has to Jesus Christ. Every man has the same relationship to his wife as Christ has to His bride, the church. Eve was made
of Adam's flesh and bone; the church is composed of the Lord's
flesh and bones. Both men and women are part of His mystical body.
"For we are members of his body, of his flesh, and of his bones"
(Ephesians 5:30).

Eve was taken from Adam's body while he slept, and so the
church was taken from the side of Christ. "But one of the soldiers
with a spear pierced his side, and forthwith came there out blood
and water" (John 19:34). That blood and water are the everlasting

71

symbols of the true church, since we are redeemed by the precious blood of Christ and washed with water by His Word (*see* 1 Peter 1:18, 19; Ephesians 5:25, 26). Blood and water are involved in the natural birth of every human, and they are involved when we are supernaturally born again.

Now what is the sole purpose of the Lord's church? Is it not to serve Him and to glorify Him on the earth? Is it not to beget children unto Him and care for them as they grow to spiritual maturity? In accordance with the scriptural parallel, does not the woman have the same responsibilities to her husband? Brethren, as a member of the body of Christ, a Christian woman is called to glorify her Lord, but when she marries, she must also glorify her husband, which is her God-given role (*see* 1 Corinthians 11:7).

Woman lost her equality with man in the garden (*see* Genesis 3:16). However, she is saved or "rewarded" in childbearing (*see* 1 Timothy 2:15). This means that God has compensated woman's loss with something wonderful, something that man can never share! God always makes all things work together for good to them that love Him, so He has made the travail of giving birth woman's greatest blessing! He makes the pain that she bears worth it all. Even as our Lord Jesus counted His suffering for us, "the joy that was set before him" (Hebrews 12:2), only the woman can so identify with Him in the water and the blood. Her suffering in childbirth is rewarded by the adoration of her husband and the children that "arise up, and call her blessed"(Proverbs 31:28).

The Scriptures teach further that all women, whether they ever have children or not, are rewarded in the miracle of the birth of the Savior, for He was born of woman with no help from man. "But when the fulness of the time was come, God sent forth his Son, made of a woman" (Galatians 4:4). All women are especially blessed, even as Mary was blessed, not *above* all women, but "among women" (*see* Luke 1:28).

In Christ there is "neither male nor female" (*see* Galatians 3:28). We are both equally important to Him, and someday all who believe and are trusting in Jesus as Savior of the body will be glorified. We will be resurrected from the earth and transformed from our present sinful flesh into the image and likeness of God forever.

32
Mother

Written to my mom when she was still with us

Mother, I love you for memories we share.
Together we've traveled a way
That was hard, and I'm grateful for all your care,
More grateful than words can e'er say.

Thanks for the prayers you have spoken for me,
For the prayer that you taught me to speak,
For bearing my burdens so willingly
When I was the one who was weak.

Thanks for a childhood of pleasures complete,
For teaching me right over wrong,
For the words that forever shall guide my feet
Through the years as I journey along.

And Mother, don't ever think I shall forget
Little joys that together we've known,
For tears you have shed, I'm forever in debt,
For the love in your smile alone.

Thank God for a Mother as faithful and true,
As reverent and sure of the right,
As firm and sincere in her ways as you,
It gives a man courage and might.

Someday you must leave me, and I shall be sad,
Not for you, for I know your reward,
But oh, how I'll miss you until the day glad
We're together again with the Lord.

33
Thanksgiving

Be thankful unto him, and bless his name.

Psalms 100:4

Thanksgiving should be a holy day when we give thanks to our Creator, not only for the blessings of life, but for the surety of His existence. How wonderful to know there is One watching over us who knows when even a sparrow falls. God loves His fallen human masterpiece more than sparrows. He loves us so much that He sent His Son to die in our place. He is not satisfied to be God only—He wants to be our heavenly Father.

On this Thanksgiving let us give thanks for the confirmation of these truths. Let us give thanks for the One whom God has appointed, the Savior of mankind.

A Thanksgiving Prayer

Thank You, Lord, for the evidence of You
In the world around us,
For the sea and sky in breathless hue
That timelessly astound us.
Thank You for the earth,
The miracle of birth,
For verdant valleys, mountain views,
For flowers that surround us.

Thank You for the starry host of heaven
Which declare Your glory,
As no pen could write nor words of men
Could ever tell the story.
For life, for joy and light,
For every restful night,

Thank You for minds to comprehend
Your silent oratory.

Thank You for loving all mankind
Despite our sin-filled ways,
For assurance that You know and mind
Our griefs and troubled days.
For mercy and for grace
To all our sins erase.
We know You hear and hold most dear
The penitent who prays.

Thank You for the Bible, Lord, each day
We search Your Word of love,
Whereby we know Your holy will and way
The truth we're certain of.
And for the Living Word,
Our Savior and our Lord,
The Word made flesh, our guide and stay
Till carried safe above.

Thank You for our yesterdays, and now
For blessings You have planned.
Thank You for the trials You allow
To help us understand.
For strength You have supplied,
For loved ones by our side.
And, Lord, we pray, bless and endow
America, our land.

34
The Efficacy of the Blood

For the life of the flesh is in the blood: and I have given it to you upon the altar to make an atonement for your souls: for it is the blood that maketh an atonement for the soul.
Leviticus 17:11

This little-known verse in the Bible is probably the most important verse in the Bible. It explains the way of salvation, the only way that sin can be atoned for. The New Testament bears out this all-important truth: "and without shedding of blood is no remission" (Hebrews 9:22).

"Forasmuch as ye know that ye were not redeemed with corruptible things, as silver and gold . . . But with the precious blood of Christ" (1 Peter 1:18, 19).

I don't understand how the blood of Jesus Christ shed on a Roman cross can save me from my sins, but I know it has! I know there is power to save in the blood of Christ because the Word of God tells us so.

The Holy Spirit of God gave wisdom to Moses, the human author of Leviticus, that was never known to his peers. Men in the time of Moses knew nothing of the physiology of the blood. Certainly they knew even less of God's plan of redemption through the shed blood of our Lord Jesus Christ. But the redeemed of the Old Testament were obedient anyway: They brought their sacrifices of lambs, bulls, and goats to the tabernacle and the temple even though they didn't understand it all.

Modern science has since learned that the life of the flesh is indeed in the blood. It is the blood in our bodies that sustains life, nothing else. In the normal human body there are about five quarts of blood. Pumped by the heart, it circulates through the system about every twenty-three seconds. It supplies every cell in our bodies with nourishment and carries away the waste products of metabolism. If the blood should fail to reach the cells and members of the body, they will promptly die.

Since the invention of the microscope we have learned much about this mysterious fluid. Much is still a mystery, but we know now that blood consists of a colorless liquid, plasma, in which are suspended various cellular elements containing many chemical compounds. Included are the red cells, about 5 million in each cubic millimeter of blood, which carry oxygen and give the blood its red color. In addition, there are white cells that defend the body against infection. They normally occur in concentrations of four to seven thousand per cubic millimeter, but their numbers miraculously and rapidly increase in case of emergency. They have the power to engulf and kill the germs in our body, though they perish in the effort.

As essential as blood is to our human bodies, so the blood of Christ is to His spiritual body, the church. Every single member of His body is saved and kept by the power of His blood. Born again into the family of God, we are all related by the same blood. It gives life, it nourishes, and it cleanses us while we are yet in Adam's likeness.

Our own blood is corruptible, and so our bodies must someday die, but the blood of Christ is incorruptible, so we can be sure that our redemption is eternal. The spiritual man is kept by the power of His sinless blood, and someday we will be given new bodies like that of our resurrected Savior. We shall be like Him at last, and the power of sin shall never touch us again.

We know that the blood of bulls and goats can never take away sin. They were only examples of the true sacrifice to be revealed later. The Old Testament saints were redeemed and kept by the blood of Christ, as we are. They are saved because they believed the promises of God, although they were not yet fulfilled. We in the church age can look back on God's finished work where the sinless blood of Jesus Christ was shed for all mankind, and it avails today for all who will accept God's unspeakable gift!

"Neither by the blood of goats and calves, but by his own blood he entered in once into the holy place, having obtained eternal redemption for us" (Hebrews 9:12).

All human blood is corruptible because of sin. When Adam sinned, he died spiritually and began to die physically that very day. God said that Adam must return to the dust of the earth from which he came. Had he not sinned, he could have lived forever. If Adam began to die from the moment he sinned, and if the life of the flesh is in the blood, then it remains *that it was Adam's blood that was. originally contaminated by sin.* Afterward, the children that were born of Adam were not born in the image and likeness of God, because they had Adam's corruptible blood.

"And Adam lived an hundred and thirty years, and begat a son in his own likeness, after his image; and called his name Seth" (Genesis 5:3).

The blood that flows in an unborn baby's arteries and veins is not derived from the mother. It is produced in the fetus only after the introduction of the male sperm. An unfertilized ovum can never develop blood; the male element develops blood and adds life, for the life of the flesh is in the blood.

This is why it was necessary for Jesus Christ to be born of a virgin, so He would have none of Adam's corruptible blood in His veins. God prepared for the virgin birth of His Son from the foundation of the world. He created woman in such a way that none of her sinful blood should ever pass from her to her unborn child. It must be created by the father and isolated in the child. Conception by the Holy Ghost was the only way the virgin birth could be accomplished. Mary contributed the body of Jesus, but the Holy Spirit of God contributed His divine and precious blood!

It is the divine blood of Jesus Christ that has power to atone for the sins of all believers—past, present, and future. The altar was a roughly hewn Roman cross, but from that cross the shed blood of Jesus Christ, flowing from His head, His hands, His side, and His feet, cleanses us from all our sins. I don't understand it all, but I believe it with all my heart.

All praise, honor, and glory then unto Him who "loved us, and washed us from our sins in his own blood" (Revelation 1:5).

35
What Is Truth?

O praise the Lord, all ye nations: praise him, all ye people.
For his merciful kindness is great toward us: and the truth of
the Lord endureth for ever. Praise ye the Lord.

Psalms 117

"What is truth?" Pilate asked the question. Our Lord answered it in His high priestly prayer to God the Father: "thy word is truth" (John 17:17). Jesus also told His disciples, "ye shall know the truth, and the truth shall make you free" (John 8:32).

Webster's dictionary defines truth as the "state or quality of being true, conformity with fact, reality or actual existence." I think *reality* fits best. Truth is something genuine and real. Adam and Eve knew truth in the beginning. They had fellowship with God, their Creator. They walked and talked with Him. They were perhaps more aware of His reality than any humans who ever lived. Made in the image and likeness of God, they could have lived in Eden forever had they not, in one weak moment, believed the lies of Satan, who urged them to disbelieve and disobey God.

Adam and Eve learned, as all men will eventually learn, that God is the Father and author of truth. Satan is the father and author of lies and ignorance. God has made known the truth to mankind in all His dealings with them. His Word was given to men by angels, by His ancient prophets, by Old Testament saints, by the psalmists, and by Moses, the lawgiver. "Holy men of God spake as they were moved by the Holy Ghost" (2 Peter 1:21).

All they wrote was ultimately confirmed by Jesus Christ, the fulfillment of God's promises and the law. Jesus Christ proved by His birth, His life, His death, and His resurrection that the ancient writings, which we call the Old Testament, are true. He is the Word of truth made flesh.

In the New Testament portion of our Bible, the apostles and certain disciples of our Lord wrote for our edification the reality of

79

Jesus Christ as the living Word of God. "That which was from the beginning, which we have heard, which we have seen with our eyes, which we have looked upon, and our hands have handled, of the Word of life" (1 John 1:1). What more could God have done to prove the truth of His Holy Word?

Men spend their lives searching for truth in science, religion, the arts, and the philosophies of other men, but they will never know genuine truth or the reality of God until they learn one basic, fundamental fact: The written Word of God, the Holy Bible, is truth! The Word of God is the only solid rock upon which a nation can build and endure. History has proved that once the Word is set aside, no civilization has ever continued to prosper.

The hypotheses and theories of men are ever changing. As we learn more and more about life, the universe, the elements that God created in the beginning, and the laws He made regarding them, we find the Bible inerrant in every respect. There is no other book like it, because it was inspired by God. It is sacred and holy, our most precious earthly possession.

The Bible provides the answers to all the mysteries of life. It explains the way of salvation. It is food for our souls as we grow to spiritual maturity. It is our authority for sound doctrine. We are instructed by God to read it prayerfully so that the Holy Spirit will help us to rightly divide it and apply the lessons to our everyday lives. The Holy Bible is the only infallible source of truth in all the physical universe!

God wrote it.
Christ proved it.
I believe it.
And that settles it!

36

Sugar-Coated Religion

Not every one that saith unto me, Lord, Lord, shall enter into the kingdom of heaven; but he that doeth the will of my Father which is in heaven. Many will say to me in that day, Lord, Lord, have we not prophesied in thy name? and in thy name have cast out devils? and in thy name done many wonderful works? And then will I profess unto them, I never knew you: depart from me, ye that work iniquity.

Matthew 7:21-23

These words from the lips of our Lord are terrifying to me! The realization that there are those in the community of Christians who actually believe they are saved but in reality are still lost and on the way to eternal hell should cause much sober, self-examination in the mind of every child of God.

Note that they call Jesus "Lord," they have performed miracles in His name, and they have done many wonderful works. The only explanation for their blindness is the deceitfulness of Satan. We must not forget that he also has the power to perform miracles. He is the great deceiver, and religion is one of his favorite weapons!

I am concerned that all of a sudden it has become the popular thing to be born again. Didn't our Lord say to His little band of genuine believers, "In the world ye shall have tribulation" (John 16:33), and did not the Apostle James warn us, "whosoever therefore will be a friend of the world is the enemy of God" (James 4:4)? Whenever our Christian testimony becomes acceptable to this world system (where Satan is prince), then there is something terribly wrong.

I am concerned about the billions of dollars being made in the name of Christianity in America today, while our overseas missionaries have so little. Never before have there been so many books written by popular and even notorious public figures about their conversion experiences. Hollywood is also getting involved, because all of a sudden the spiritual and the occult are the "in things"! Never before have there been so many "gospel" singers and musicians playing before such huge audiences and on prime-time television. The sales of their gospel records and tapes bring in hundreds of millions of dollars annually. Never before have there been so many radio and television evangelists pleading for more of our money to continue their "good works." Brethren, so much of it smacks of big business!

Meanwhile the moral climate in the United States continues its roller-coaster descent. Never before have Americans been exposed to such filth as that shown on television and in the movies today. Never before have we experienced the vulgarity and indecency displayed in the literature that we read. Our courts can no longer even define pornography. Nor can the law do anything to stem the satanic tide of fornication, adultery, abortion, terrorism, homosexuality, and the flagrant disregard of the rights of those members of society who still want to live separated, decent, honorable, Godfearing lives!

When we consider this strange paradox—the great increase in religious interest and its acceptance by an increasingly vile society—we cannot help but fear there is something terribly wrong! Where is the fruit of the "good works" so acclaimed?

The Word of God tells us that in the last days there will be a lukewarm church with no power. It will be popular because it will set aside annoying doctrines. There will be no further references to eternal hell or to the fact that we are all sinners who must be saved. There will be little mention of the power of the blood of Jesus Christ. Old-fashioned repentance will not be preached from the pulpits of these "enlightened" congregations.

I cannot help but wonder whether some of this new generation of "believers" really have their feet planted on the Rock of their salvation. I wonder if they haven't rather been coaxed into a profession of faith in Jesus Christ by a watered-down, sugar-coated religion that promises them fame, fortune, and success through the simple expedient of believing. I wonder if they really know all that is involved in believing on the Lord Jesus Christ, or if they have ever counted the cost of being genuine disciples of our Lord. I wonder why so many of these converts are not interested in being baptized and getting involved in the work of the local church. I wonder why they espouse the love of God but cannot endure sound doctrine. I wonder if they will still be able to stand when the storms come.

Brethren, our Lord never promised us a rose garden; not in this life. He said the world would hate us because it hated Him. If we really believe in Him, we will probably never be called successful by this world's standards, because we will want to live to His glory and not our own. However, living for Jesus brings a peace and inner joy that this world knows little of. Our success is measured in things eternal. Our blessed hope is not in the things of this world but in the rapture of being caught up to meet Him in the air and hearing Him say, "Well done, thou good and faithful servants."

37
Definition of a Christian

I said, "Are you a Christian?"
He stared, and answered then,
"This is a Christian nation,
And I am a citizen.

"Yes, I believe in God,
I practice the Golden Rule,
And when I was a youngster,
I went to Sunday school.

"I've got a Bible somewhere
That my mother used to read.
I believe all men are equal
Despite their race or creed."

"Do you go to church?" I asked.
"Well, frankly, no," he said.
"We're out so late on Saturday
I usually stay in bed.

"But I believe in churches, yes,
I think they look so nice,
And I contribute now and then
To combat crime and vice."

"And do you pray?" I questioned.
He said, "You bet I do;
I really prayed in '29,
And once when I had the flu.

"Sure, I'm a Christian, buddy,
And I do all I can,
So now if you'll excuse me,
I'm a very busy man."

38
What Is a Hypocrite?

One who makes a display of virtues he does not really possess.
Webster

A Christian cannot be a hypocrite, for in order to be a Christian, we must first of all recognize that we are sinners. The next step is to confess our sins and to accept God's forgiveness through faith in Jesus Christ. Christians then are *saved* sinners. We do not automatically stop sinning when we become Christians, though with God's help, we do improve. The only virtue we claim is that of Christ, not of ourselves.

The hypocrite refuses to admit that he is a sinner. He feels no real need for Christ or for the church, even though he may attend some kind of church that does not offend his conscience. He claims virtue that he does not possess.

The Bible says that *all* have sinned and *all* continue to come short of the glory of God. It says—even to the Christian—that if we say we have no sin, we deceive ourselves and the truth is not in us.

Therefore, there are only two types of people in the world: *saved* sinners and *lost* sinners. Which are you? And who is the real hypocrite?

39
The Eyes of the World

It's easy to look like a Christian.
Being pious is not such an art,
For the world cannot peer
'Neath the pretty veneer
Of the sin-blackened, selfish heart.

Going to church every Sunday
And placing a gift on the plate
Is an easy way out,
And the world cannot doubt,
Though the soul may be steeped with hate.

Fasting, abstaining, continually praying
May win many plaudits abroad,
But a fool cannot hide
What is written inside
From the eyes of a watchful God!

40

What Does It Mean to Believe?

Believe on the Lord Jesus Christ, and thou shalt be saved, and thy house.

Acts 16:31

The English language cannot adequately describe in one word all that it means and all that takes place when we believe on the Lord Jesus Christ. The above verse is so often quoted but so little understood. We are reminded that the Apostle James wrote, "the devils also believe, and tremble" (James 2:19).

Acquiescence to the truth and to the reality of Jesus Christ is not enough. Nor is "head knowledge" of Christ and the Bible enough. There are many who believe that Christ is real and that the Bible is true, who may still be unsaved. Consequently, we hear some Christian teachers add that we must also "accept" Jesus Christ. This is true, but this is also another overused and seldom-explained word in our Christian vocabulary. We need to hear more about all that is involved in "believing on" and "accepting" Jesus Christ. We need to know with assurance that we have indeed been born again into the family and household of God, and we need to know *how* this occurs!

Believing on Jesus Christ involves the entire plan and finished work of God for redeeming the lost human soul. *It means going through the complete conversion experience.* It is not enough to know that we are redeemed by the precious blood of Jesus Christ shed on a Roman cross. We need to know how that blood can be applied to us, personally.

The Word of God tells us that the miracle of salvation involves the work of God the Holy Spirit; the sacrifice of Jesus Christ the Son; the grace of God the Father; and the obedient but sweet surrender of the individual human will. It is the most wonderful event in human experience, superseded only by the rapture, when we shall see God face-to-face. Those so born again are made new creatures and henceforth live supernatural lives!

The Bible teaches that the following steps of salvation are requisite experiences that every true child of God can recall. We are assured by the Word of God that these things must take place, and by them we know that we are on our way to heaven.

We Are Called

No one comes to Christ until He first calls them. The truly saved can recall the time or times when God the Holy Spirit appealed to them regarding their lost condition. It may have been through the spoken or written words of a Christian friend, a pastor, or a teacher. It may have come through reading the Bible. It may have occurred after observing the peace and joy in the lives of others who know the Lord. It may have been the culmination of many observations and experiences, but somehow, one day, the still, small voice of God spoke, and we knew that it was real.

The Philippian jailer to whom the foregoing Scripture was addressed had witnessed the joy of Paul and Silas as they sang of their Redeemer, even though they had been beaten, cast into a dungeon, and shackled! He witnessed the power of God when an earthquake shook the prison and opened the doors of the cells. He witnessed the faith of Paul and Silas as they stayed in their cells and did not seek to escape. God the Holy Spirit used all these ways to call this man to Himself. The church (*ekklesia*) is a "called out" assembly. "Moreover whom he did predestinate, them he also called" (Romans 8:30).

We Are Convicted

When we are called by God the Holy Spirit, we come under conviction. We recognize that we are sinners unworthy of the holy love of God. Only this Spirit-induced, genuine conviction can lead us to accept God's forgiveness.

We can also be convicted and do nothing about it. The Word of God tells us clearly that unsaved sinners will go to hell, and there are untold millions who have been convicted of this truth but have still refused to take the next step to salvation. The Bible tells us they harden their hearts and that there will come a day when the Holy Spirit will no longer plead with them!

The Philippian jailer was under conviction as he came trembling to fall down before Paul and Silas. He asked, "What must I do to be saved?" He was ready to take the next step. He not only believed "in" the Lord Jesus Christ, he was now ready to believe "on" Him! "And when he [the Holy Spirit] is come, he will reprove [convict] the world of sin" (John 16:8).

We Confess We Are Sinners and Repent

If we are unwilling to confess our sins, we cannot be saved, nor could we ever live the Christian life. Christians grow spiritually as they become convicted of sin in their lives and are willing to confess it. "If we confess our sins, he is faithful and just to forgive us our sins, and to cleanse us from all unrighteousness" (1 John 1:9).

We not only confess our sins, but in the same breath we repent of them. This means we have a change of mind and heart that completely changes us. We no longer consider ourselves as good as anyone else, and we recognize how far short we come of the glory of God. Our attitude toward God and our fellowman is changed by the ever-convicting power of the Holy Spirit.

We make restitution for our past sins whenever possible, and we ask God's help in the continuing battle with Satan, the lust of the flesh, and sin. The Philippian jailer showed his repentance by taking Paul and Silas into his own house and washing their stripes.

We Are Obedient

When the Apostle Peter preached to the people after the miracle of Pentecost, they were convicted. They were . . .

pricked in their heart, and said unto Peter and to the rest of the apostles, Men and brethren, what shall we do? Then Peter said unto them, Repent, and be baptized every one of you in the name of Jesus Christ for the remission of sins, and ye shall receive the gift of the Holy Ghost. For the promise is unto you, and to your children, and to all that are afar off, even as many as the Lord our God shall call.

Acts 2:37-39

Brethren, the first step of obedience is water baptism. It is recorded for our edification again and again in the New Testament that believers were immediately baptized. The Lord Himself submitted to a sinner's baptism to identify Himself with us. And God said, "This is my beloved Son, in whom I am well pleased" (Matthew 3:17). We in turn are commanded to submit to baptism to denote our identity with Him. Baptism is our public confession of faith in Christ, and it demonstrates that we are not ashamed of our new identity.

Paul and Silas went through the entire plan of salvation with the Philippian jailer and his family. They explained all that it means to believe on the Lord Jesus Christ. "And they spake unto him the word of the Lord, and to all that were in his house. And he took them the same hour of the night, and washed their stripes; and was baptized, he and all his, straightway" (Acts 16:32, 33).

We born-again believers continue to be obedient. We feed on the "sincere milk of the word, that ye may grow thereby" (1 Peter 2:2). We "study to shew thyself approved unto God, a workman that needeth not to be ashamed, rightly dividing the word of truth" (2 Timothy 2:15). And we surrender our bodies as our reasonable service to the use of God's Holy Spirit (*see* Romans 12:1). We seek to know our Father's will, and we are obedient to His plans for our own particular lives. We do our best to keep the commandments of our Lord, and in so doing, we find life's greatest fulfillment. We come to realize that our greatest joy is in pleasing Him.

Jesus said, "And why call ye me Lord, Lord, and do not the things which I say?" (Luke 6:46). *Brethren, it is by our obedience that we make the Savior our Lord.*

This is at least part of all it means to "believe on the Lord Jesus Christ." These are only the first steps of the whole wonderful Christian experience, but by them we know that we are His!

41

One of the Gang

It's great to be known as one of the gang,
A regular fellow, they say.
You're one of the best,
If you do as the rest,
Enthused, as you follow their way.

It's smart to gamble, if other folks
Endorse its enjoyments aloud.
Rolling the dice
Is worth any price
If it's done by the rest of the crowd.

It's proper to drink all the popular brands,
And lie in the gutter at night,
They'll giggle and say,
As they go on their way,
That you are a "bit of all right."

You'll never be branded a square or a nut
If you haven't a mind of your own,
If you're "hep" to the ways
Of the latest craze,
You're clever, and never alone.

But God needs men who want purpose in life,
Undeterred by the worldly harangue
To conform to the norm
And avoid every storm
By becoming "just one of the gang."

"But ye are a chosen generation, a royal priesthood, an holy nation, a peculiar people; that ye should shew forth the praises of him who hath called you out of darkness into his marvellous light" (1 Peter 2:9).

42

The Successful Life

*I have seen all the works that are done under the sun; and,
behold, all is vanity and vexation of spirit.*

Ecclesiastes 1:14

Sometimes we wonder just what life is all about, anyway. Everyone is eager for words of wisdom regarding life. They are willing to sit at the feet of a successful man. They want to learn the secret of his success.

By this world's standards, the most successful man who ever lived was King Solomon of Israel, the author of many wise proverbs and the Book of Ecclesiastes. The world should pay heed to what Solomon has to say!

Solomon, as a young king, prayed to God for wisdom and an understanding heart, that he might rule his people well. It was a prayer that so pleased the Lord that He not only gave him unparalleled wisdom, but also great riches and honors. So Solomon reigned during Israel's greatest prosperity, and the fame of Solomon exceeded that of all men.

God allowed him to build the temple, an honor that was denied to King David, his father. It was the most splendid building on earth. The temple and Solomon's own palace were both magnificent structures, richly decorated and overlaid with pure gold. There has been nothing to equal them in the history of the world.

Solomon devoted much time and study to the sciences, botany, public works, and commerce. His knowledge of many things was unmatched by his contemporaries. His amazing discourses on the hydrosphere and the atmosphere in the Book of Ecclesiastes were not taught in the universities of his day. The words of wisdom by which he spoke, his keen psychology, and the knowledge displayed in his writings were special gifts from God.

His navies gathered inestimable riches, including rare spices, timber, gold, and exotic cloth from all over the known world, which made Israel wealthy and increased her splendor. After her en-counter with Solomon, the Queen of Sheba—when she had ob-served his wisdom and seen his house, the meat on his table, his servants and ministers, their apparel, and the glorious House of the Lord—said, "It was a true report that I heard in mine own land of thy acts and of thy wisdom. Howbeit I believed not the words, until I came, and mine eyes had seen it: and, behold, the half was not told me" (1 Kings 10:6, 7).

Brethren, by this world's standards, King Solomon was indeed the most successful man who ever lived. He really put it all together! But he had some sober reflections regarding what life is all about. All his fame, wisdom, and riches did *not* bring him the peace of mind and happiness he thought they would. Again and again in his writings, he lamented, "Vanity of vanities, all is vanity."

Solomon learned, as no other man has had such an opportunity to learn, that we are not to labor for things that perish. Our Lord Jesus said, "Consider the lilies of the field, how they grow; they toil not, neither do they spin: And yet I say unto you, That even Solomon in all his glory was not arrayed like one of these" (Matthew 6:28, 29). What did Jesus mean? What was it that Solomon had over-looked regarding the joy of living?

Solomon provides us with the answers himself. He explains that he assumed he would find the real meaning of life through wisdom. But rather than satisfaction, wisdom brought him grief and the ultimate conclusion that all the works of man under the sun are but "vanity and vexation of spirit." He learned that man who lives only for the transitory things of this life will find that knowledge in-creaseth sorrow!

Solomon learned that *without God there is no hope for mankind,* even as wise men today see nothing ahead but the eventual destruc-tion of the human race. Our scientists tell us that we are out of fuel, air, water, and time. If total atomic war doesn't destroy us, our own atmosphere most certainly will! The Apostle Paul wrote, "If in this life only we have hope in Christ, we are of all men most miserable" (1 Corinthians 15:19).

But we have a greater hope! We who know Jesus Christ as our Savior and Lord are given, like Solomon, a wisdom from above. Our faith is not in the works of our hands, but in God and in His eternal Word. Our hope is in the finished work of Jesus Christ. We know that He lives and that He is coming again. We have seen the promises of God fulfilled in the life, death, and resurrection of our Lord, and now our feet are upon the Solid Rock! This kind of wisdom brings peace amid the conflict all around us. This kind of wisdom allows us to accept and enjoy the transitory things of this life by putting them into their proper perspective.

Solomon learned that wisdom and knowledge and possessions, apart from a right relationship with God, are not sufficient. But when God is feared, we can make all of life rewarding to ourselves, a blessing to our neighbors, and a sweet-smelling savor to the Lord.

Solomon learned that the secret of a successful life is not in earning the plaudits of the world, but in giving God first place in all that we think or do. Without God all is "vanity and vexation of spirit," but when our works glorify Him, our spiritual nature is rewarded and experiences *great exultation!* Solomon has written, "The fear of the Lord is the beginning of knowledge: but fools despise wisdom and instruction" (Proverbs 1:7).

What makes a man successful? First, a right relationship with his Creator. In the Dispensation of Grace, it is called the New Birth. Then, if we are obedient to our calling, we begin the truly rewarding, wonderful adventure of living for Jesus Christ until He calls us home! This is wisdom. Then, as we acquire knowledge, we can apply it with eternity's values in mind.

What is life all about? Well, for those outside the family of God, it is vanity, culminating in hell and the lake of fire that is God's final judgment of the works of man! But to those who accept God's priceless gift of salvation and eternal life, it is peace and joy and reward even in the midst of trials, and praise God, we can look forward to an eternity of happiness, where there will be no more trials. It means looking forward to the new heavens and the new earth which we will someday inherit.

Brethren, God is on the throne. Don't ever doubt it. He has a plan for your life and for my life. He is preparing us for *eternity!* And we should know that the blessings of this life and the trials of this life are needful for us and for our loved ones. As members of the body of Christ we are, therefore, exhorted to share our joys and our sorrows, to pray for and comfort one another until our work on earth is at last complete and God takes us home.

For the Lord himself shall descend from heaven with a shout with the voice of the archangel, and with the trump of God:

and the dead in Christ shall rise first: Then we which are alive and remain shall be caught up together with them in the clouds, to meet the Lord in the air: and so shall we ever be with the Lord. Wherefore comfort one another with these words.

1 Thessalonians 4:16-18

And that is what life is all about! King Solomon, the wisest of all earthlings, concluded his ponderings with these words: "Let us hear the conclusion of the whole matter: Fear God, and keep his commandments: for this is the whole duty of man" (Ecclesiastes 12:13).

43
Definition of a Successful Man

What makes a man successful?
What standard can we plan
Applicable to measure
The performance of a man

Is it the great attainments
Of fortune, lands, or fame?
Is it found in simple dignity,
Or in honors that we claim?

Is not the simplest standard
One that when to all applied,
Will tell if such successes
Leave the whole man satisfied?

For man is more than only mind,
More than senses to console,
Man like God is triune,
Man is spirit, body, soul.

Success must then be measured
By the beauty of the three,
And man must be the kind of man
It was planned for him to be.

What makes a man successful?
It is first to seek the mind
Of the One who has designed him,
And to follow close behind.

What makes a man successful?
It is then to do his best,
And to have the peace of knowing
That the Lord will do the rest.

44

The Names of Our Lord

*His name shall be called Wonderful, Counseller, The mighty
God, The everlasting Father, The Prince of Peace.*

Isaiah 9:6

The first name given for God in the Bible in the original Hebrew
is *Elohim.* "In the beginning *Elohim* created the heaven and the
earth" (Genesis 1:1). The name implies strength or the power of
God as Creator of the universe. It is a uni-plural noun, indicative of
the Triune God, grammatically acceptable when related to a plural
pronoun, as when God said, "Let us make man in our image, after
our likeness" (Genesis 1:26).

Later, Abraham learned to know God as *Adonai,* which means
"Master" or "Lord." The name implies His proper relationship to
mankind. Adonai, as used in the Bible, also applies to the head of
the family or a slave owner.

Abraham, Isaac, and Jacob all came to know the Lord as *El
Shaddai,* which means "Almighty God."

Abraham, after his encounter with Melchizedek, knew Him as
El Elyon, which means "the Most High God."

But when the time came for God to redeem His chosen people,
Israel, from their bondage in Egypt, He then chose to reveal His
most holy name! This name, which we can write with the four
English letters *YHWH,* has never been pronounced by the Jews
because of their reverence for the sacredness of that divine name.
The ancient Hebrew scribes would reverently wipe their pens whenever they copied any of the names for God, but when they came to
this name, they were commanded to wash their entire bodies!

This holy but seemingly unpronounceable name has been con-
sistently transliterated as *Yahweh* or *Jehovah.* Recognizing now that
there is no scholarly excuse for this, the more recent translators are
using LORD whenever YHWH occurs in the original Hebrew. The
only exception to this is when YHWH occurs in immediate

proximity to *Adonai,* which has already been translated "Lord." In this case YHWH is translated "God" to avoid confusion. Thus *Adonai YHWH* is translated in the latest Bibles as "LORD God."

None of the translations convey the true meaning of that wonderful name and all it was intended to convey to those whom God would more intimately reveal Himself. Let me share with you the Scriptures in which God so made Himself known to Moses. It will clarify the meaning of the name and help us understand its ultimate purpose.

"And God said unto Moses, I AM THAT I AM: and he said, Thus shalt thou say unto the children of Israel, I AM hath sent me unto you" (Exodus 3:14).

"And God spake unto Moses, and said unto him, I am the Lord: And I appeared unto Abraham, unto Isaac, and unto Jacob by the name of God Almighty, but by my name Jehovah was I not known to them" (Exodus 6: 2, 3).

God also spoke to the prophet Isaiah regarding His most holy name when He said, "I am the LORD: that is my name: and my glory will I not give to another, neither my praise to graven images" (Isaiah 42:8).

Therefore, the best translation of the wonderful name is "I AM, or The Eternally Existent One." Furthermore, the compound use of that name in the Holy Scriptures magnifies the meaning so that we can literally interpret it as "I AM or The Eternally Existent One who progressively and more intimately reveals Himself to His own."

Let me explain: The name YHWH is first used in connection with the planned redemption of a nation, but in a larger sense it has to do with the redemption of all the people of God from the bondage of sin. It is to the redeemed that God progressively reveals Himself in the Holy Scriptures, and by the compound use of His most holy name, He more intimately reveals Himself in special redeemer relationships to all His holy family. Also, it is through the compound use of this name that we know that Jesus Christ, our Savior and Lord, is the I AM of the Old Testament! Consider the following precious Scriptures: "And Abraham said, My son, God will provide himself a lamb for a burnt offering" (Genesis 22:8).

"And Abraham called the name of that place Jehovah-jireh" (Genesis 22:14).

Jehovah-jireh is the first of these compound names and is best translated, "I AM will provide [the sacrifice]." And brethren, did not John the Baptist proclaim of Jesus, "Behold the Lamb of God, which taketh away the sin of the world"(John 1:29)?

Other compound uses of His wonderful name are:

Jehovah-rapha (I AM who heals: Exodus 15:26). Very early in His earthly ministry, our Lord demonstrated His power to heal. He is the great healer of both the souls and bodies of them that love Him.

Jehovah-nissi (I AM, our banner: Exodus 17:15). It is Jesus who is our banner and protector. We go forth in His name, and He has promised that He will never leave us nor forsake us (*see* Hebrews 13:5).

Jehovah-shalom (I AM, our peace: Judges 6:24). Our Lord Jesus is the Prince of Peace. He said, "my peace I give unto you" (John 14:27).

Jehovah-raah (I AM, our shepherd: Psalms 23). Jesus said of Himself, "I am the good shepherd: the good shepherd giveth his life for the sheep" (John 10:11).

Jehovah-tsidkenu (I AM, our righteousness: Jeremiah 23:6). All of our righteousness is as filthy rags, but "Christ is made unto us righteousness" (*see* 1 Corinthians 1:30). "For he hath made him to be sin for us, who knew no sin; that we might be made the righteousness of God in him" (2 Corinthians 5:21).

Jehovah-shammah (I AM, present with us: Ezekiel 48:35). The promise in the Old Testament is, of course, first given to Israel, but Jesus said to His disciple and us, "Lo, I am with you alway, even unto the end of the world" (Matthew 28:20).

These seven compound names (seven is the number of completeness in the Bible) give us a complete picture of our Lord in His redeemer relationship. How sad that much of the meaning of these Hebrew words is lost in our modern translations, for I believe that God intended these progressive revelations of Himself to culminate in the revelation of Jesus Christ!

Jesus said to the Jews, "Your father Abraham rejoiced to see my day: and he saw it, and was glad" (John 8:56). This must have occurred when Abraham had demonstrated his willingness to sacrifice his son in obedience to God, but was prevented by the voice of an angel. It was then that Abraham learned that I AM would provide a lamb for the sacrifice and that ultimately, I AM would provide the only acceptable sacrifice for the sins of the whole world!

"Then said the Jews unto him, Thou art not fifty years old, and hast thou seen Abraham? Jesus said unto them, Verily, verily, I say unto you, Before Abraham was, I am" (John 8:57, 58).

The prophet Isaiah declared that His name should be called *Immanuel,* meaning "God present with us." And so He is—the holy I AM embodied in human flesh; first in the likeness of the Son of man and now in His glorified body as the firstfruits of a great harvest yet to come, yet still present with us by His Holy Spirit.

And then, in the last book of the Bible, the Revelation of Jesus Christ, our Lord leaves no doubt that He is the Eternally Existent One as he declares: "I am Alpha and Omega, the beginning and the ending . . . which is, and which was, and which is to come, the Almighty" (Revelation 1:8).

Brethren, Jesus Christ literally fulfilled God's progressive revelation of Himself in every detail. There was no doubt in the minds of the apostles, as they began their ministry, that Jesus Christ was God, the Elohim, Adonai, El Shaddai, El Elyon, and the I AM of the Old Testament. They proclaimed this great truth with boldness.

The Apostle John wrote: "In the beginning was the Word, and the Word was with God, and the Word was God" (John 1:1).

The Apostle Peter concluded his first sermon with this declaration: "Therefore let all the house of Israel know assuredly, that God hath made that same Jesus, whom ye have crucified, both Lord and Christ" (Acts 2:36).

Paul wrote: "For it pleased the Father that in him [the Son] should all fulness [of the Godhead] dwell" (Colossians 1:19).

Finally, compare with me the following astounding declarations from the Old and New Testaments; first from the Old Testament, leaving in the names of God as written in the original Hebrew:

For thus saith the I AM that created the heavens; Elohim himself that formed the earth and made it; he hath established it, he created it not in vain, he formed it to be inhabited: I AM; and there is none else. Tell ye, and bring them near; yea, let them take counsel together: who hath declared this from ancient time? who hath told it from that time? have not I the YHWH [I AM]? and there is no Elohim else beside me; a just El Shaddai and a Saviour; there is none beside me. Look unto me, and be ye saved, all the ends of the earth: for I am El [the Mighty One], and there is none else. I have sworn by myself, the word is gone out of my mouth in righteousness, and shall not return, That unto me every knee shall bow, every tongue shall swear [confess].

Isaiah 45:18, 21-23

And from the New Testament:

Wherefore God also hath highly exalted him [Jesus], and given him a name which is above every name: That at the name of Jesus every knee should bow . . . And that every tongue should confess that Jesus Christ is Lord, to the glory of God the Father.

Philippians 2:9-11

And so it will be, brethren, when we get to heaven and see the Holy I AM face-to-face. When we shall at last see Him as He is, we will be looking into the face of Jesus, and His name to us will indeed be *wonderful!*

45

Perfect Peace

*Thou wilt keep him in perfect peace, whose mind is stayed on
thee: because he trusteth in thee.*

Isaiah 26:3

This is one of my favorite verses. It comforts trusting Christian
minds in the same manner that our guardian angels reassure our
trembling souls as they "encampeth round about them that fear him,
and delivereth them" (Psalms 34:7). Yet its true meaning is so little
understood.

God never promised us that we would not experience stress or
emotional upset or tribulation. He did promise us His peace, the
peace that brought Him through His own sufferings. He said:
"Peace I leave with you, my peace I give unto you: not as the world
giveth, give I unto you. Let not your heart be troubled, neither let
it be afraid" (John 14:27).

"These things I have spoken unto you, that in me ye might have
peace. In the world ye shall have tribulation: but be of good cheer;
I have overcome the world" (John 16:33).

Most of the Christians I know are experiencing varying degrees
of tribulation. We are all acquainted with disappointments and
sorrow. And I'm just about out of patience with those television
evangelists and their seemingly hypnotized, overexuberant followers who are continually espousing their blessings of health,
wealth, and happiness because they have more faith than I! The
most faithful and dedicated Christians this world has ever known
have suffered for their faith, and many have been martyred. All
Christians have a cross to bear. We all have unsaved loved ones and
friends who seemingly will not come to Christ, and if we sincerely
care, we must weep for them.

Some of the most faithful of God's children are experiencing
serious illnesses and pain for which we have no explanation. Yet
their trust in God has not diminished and they have within them that

perfect peace and joy this world knows little about. It is the Lord's peace.

His peace, from my point of view, comes as we learn to keep our minds "stayed" on Him (continually directed toward Him) and from trusting in Him regardless of our trials. We know that He is sovereign and whatever He allows will ultimately "work together for good to them that love God, to them who are the called according to his purpose" (Romans 8:28).

God has a plan for every life, and all that He allows is for the sake of His elect. If we are faithful in doing our best for Him, He will most surely turn our present earthly travails into blessings for all eternity. Even when we fail Him, He will not fail us. Our primary weakness is in learning to trust Him. The patriarch Job, who suffered more than any of us ever shall, said of his tribulations, "Though he slay me, yet will I trust in him" (Job 13:15).

The "peace of God, which passeth all understanding" (Philippians 4:7) doesn't come as an instantaneous gift when we are saved. It comes as we, through many trials, learn to trust Him in all things, and most of us are hard to teach!

Whenever we're made brokenhearted,
And shrouded by clouds of despair,
When we're shaken by fears,
When we're seeing through tears,
And our hopes have all vanished in air.

When loved ones aren't able to help us,
When the battle is all our own,
Though friendships we treasure
Are sweet beyond measure,
The anguish is only our own.

The world then has nothing to offer,
Its pleasures are suddenly void,
For the cry in our heart,
Only God can impart
A peace the world never enjoyed.

Peace beyond all understanding,
And comfort beyond our belief,

His grace will reclaim us,
His strength will sustain us,
His love will conquer our grief.

Our Father who's watching in heaven
Has promised His care all the way.
His joyful tomorrow
Will make even sorrow
The circumstance needed today.

Be glad for the promise of heaven,
Be sure, for He spared not His Son,
Believe the true story,
And live for His glory,
Trust God, and the victory's won!

46

The Doctrine of Predestination

For whom he did foreknow, he also did predestinate to be conformed to the image of his Son, that he might be the firstborn among many brethren. Moreover whom he did predestinate, them he also called: and whom he called, them he also justified: and whom he justified, them he also glorified.

Romans 8:29, 30

So many of the clergy and brethren in the laity are reluctant to discuss the doctrine of predestination. Subsequently, the often asked question, "Why would a loving and just God choose some of His creation for heaven and some for hell?" goes unanswered. The same applies to another question: "Why would God create at all those whom He has predestined for destruction?" This also results in evasive answers such as, "God knows best," or "Someday we'll understand."

One of the better though unsatisfactory answers often heard is that because God is sovereign, He can do as He chooses with His creation. The supporting Scripture for this reply is: "Hath not the potter power over the clay, of the same lump to make one vessel unto honour, and another unto dishonour?" (Romans 9:21).

But this still leaves the age-old question, "Why?" unanswered.

Brethren, the answers to all our questions are provided in the Holy Scriptures, but we need to consider *all* the Scriptures regarding a subject before coming to a conclusion. My own point of view regarding predestination is supported, I believe, by all that is written in God's Word about it. Otherwise, I would not attempt to share these thoughts with you.

First, and most important, we know that it is not God's holy will that any should perish. "The Lord is not slack concerning his promise, as some men count slackness; but is longsuffering to us-ward, not willing that any should perish, but that all should come to repentance" (2 Peter 3:9).

We know that we are all sinners and none are worthy of heaven. "There is none righteous, no, not one" (Romans 3:10). And we also know that "Except a man be born again, he cannot see the kingdom of God" (John 3:3). And, "whosoever shall call on the name of the Lord shall be saved" (Acts 2:21).

With these Scriptures in mind, then, how does God choose, elect, or predestinate those who are to be conformed to the image of His Son?

It is by His foreknowledge! We who are saved are the "Elect according to the foreknowledge of God" (1 Peter 1:2). We were "chosen [in Christ] before the foundation of the world" (Ephesians 1:4). "For whom he did foreknow, he also did predestinate" (Romans 8:29).

God, therefore, did not arbitrarily predestinate some of us to be saved and some to go to eternal hell, as we have often heard predestination defined. But because He is omniscient (having all knowledge), He knew, before He ever created the world, those who would someday of their own free will call upon His name and be saved, and so He predestinated them to spend eternity with Him in the image of His firstborn! God intimately knew each one of His creation before they were ever born. He knows their names, and He knows their futures. He knows those who are already condemned and those who will spend eternity with Him. We who are saved are predestined to become His greatest masterpiece. We shall be more glorious than the angels. We shall be like Him. "And as we have borne the image of the earthy [Adam], we shall also bear the image of the heavenly [Christ]" (1 Corinthians 15:49).

Jesus said, "For many are called, but few are chosen" (Matthew 22:14). He knew that while the Gospel would be preached to all nations, not all mankind would believe. Neither will God force anyone to believe and be saved, but He has said, "whosoever believeth in him should not perish" (John 3:16). God wants us to love Him because He first loved us, and our love must be freely given. And again, because He is the I AM (not bound by the dimensions of time), He knows all those who will respond to and return His love, and He has chosen them to be His children. Their names were written in the Lamb's Book of Life before time began.

The psalmist has written:

My substance was not hid from thee, when I was made in secret, and curiously wrought in the lowest parts of the earth. Thine eyes did see my substance, yet being unperfect; and in thy book all my members were written, which in continuance were fashioned, when as yet there was none of them.

                                                        Psalms 139:15, 16

Jeremiah was told by the Lord, "Before I formed thee in the belly I knew thee; and before thou camest forth out of the womb I sanctified thee, and I ordained thee a prophet unto the nations" (Jeremiah 1:5).

And of the unsaved, God has written, "and they that dwell on the earth shall wonder, whose names were not written in the book of life from the foundation of the world" (Revelation 17:8).

"And whosoever was not found written in the book of life was cast into the lake of fire" (Revelation 20:15).

Why then were the wicked created, and why are they allowed to live? *It is for the sake of the elect.* For as the Scriptures say, "all things work together for good to them that love God" (Romans 8:28). There are tares among the wheat, as Jesus said, and they are not to be gathered until the harvest, lest the wheat be uprooted also. "Let both grow together until the harvest: and in the time of harvest I will say to the reapers, Gather ye together first the tares, and bind them in bundles to burn them: but gather the wheat into my barn" (Matthew 13:30).

It is necessary for God to allow those whom He cannot save to be born and to live for a time and for a purpose. Many of us who are saved were born of unsaved parents. God uses the unredeemable in many ways, even as Pharaoh in the Old Testament was used to demonstrate the power of God to God's foreknown and chosen nation of Israel; even as Pilate was used both to declare Jesus innocent and then to condemn Him. Remember the words of our Lord to Pilate? "Thou couldest have no power at all against me, except it were given thee from above" (John 19:11).

Even Satan was created and allowed to live for a purpose in the plan of God. But brethren, we can be sure, on the solid rock foundation of the Holy Scriptures, that someday when all the foreknown righteous are safely in the fold, God will destroy Satan.

He will judge the wicked, and all the unsaved will be cast into the lake of fire.

The good news of the Holy Gospel is that whosoever will, may come and be saved. The fact that God already knows all those who will come unto Him does not change this great truth! It does mean, however, that God must wait until all those whom He has chosen have been redeemed from this condemned world.

Our Lord Jesus came to save those chosen and predestined to eternal life by God, the Father. His shed blood has the potential to redeem the entire human race, but God knew it would not be so. He foreknew those who would believe, and He gave them to His Son. This was confirmed by Jesus in His high priestly prayer: "I have manifested thy name unto the men which thou gavest me out of the world: thine they were, and thou gavest them me; and they have kept thy word. I pray for them: I pray not for the world, but for them which thou hast given me; for they are thine" (John 17:6, 9).

And that, I believe, is the secret of the much debated doctrine of predestination.

47

Courage

What does the word *afraid* imply?
A lack of courage or the fear
Of such a lack when dangers I
Must face appear.

Is it courage that outstands
If I to risk my life would dare
By circus stunts on practiced hands
Through empty air?

Any man, now I would say,
Who just for showmanship would run,
Is not so brave, but rather a
Foolhardy one.

But if to help a friend I flee
Across some chasm of the dead
Though terrified, I still would be
A thoroughbred.

48

The Creation

In the beginning God created the heaven and the earth.

Genesis 1:1

We don't know how long ago that act of creation was, and I believe we shall never know on this side of heaven. Scientists, astronomers, and geologists foolishly speculate in hundreds of millions of years. May I point out that things are not always what they seem?

For example: It seems logical to assume that the heavens are millions of years old due to the immeasurable distances of some of the galaxies from the planet earth and the fact that it would take millions of years for their light to reach us. Is it not also logical that their Creator might have created the light rays simultaneously with the stars themselves?

Or if we could have seen Adam and Eve immediately after their creation, in the full bloom of young adulthood, would we not have assumed them to be twenty-five or thirty years of age?

We have an omnipotent God who needs only to speak and His creative work is performed.

By the word of the Lord were the heavens made, and all the host of them by the breath of his mouth. He gathereth the waters of the sea together as an heap: he layeth up the depth in storehouses. Let all the earth fear the Lord: let all the inhabitants of the world stand in awe of him. For he spake, and it was done; he commanded, and it stood fast.

Psalms 33:6-9

Our Almighty Creator doesn't have to wait for the processes of nature that He designed and controls!

I am reminded of the old riddle regarding which came first, the chicken or the egg. How foolish. Neither is logical. God had to create both a hen and a rooster first! It is ridiculous to assume that an egg could evolve and then hatch all by itself. Yet that is the very theory that some of the most learned of scientists are proposing today.

There are many, even among the family of the redeemed, who challenge the belief that God created the heaven and the earth in six days. The Bible doesn't really say that He did, but we better believe that He *could!* Let's not limit God to horizons of human perception and finite capabilities. I really get annoyed with the so-called theistic evolutionists who compromise the miracle of it all with the natural processes of nature as "God's method of creation." Brethren, if we have difficulty believing the miraculous and instantaneous power of our Creator; if we cannot believe that He could create the heaven and the earth and all that dwell therein in six days, then how are we ever going to believe God's holy promise that, "In a moment, in the twinkling of an eye" (1 Corinthians 15:52), He will raise all the saints from Adam till the end of the age, catch them up to meet Him in the air, and instantaneously transform both the living and the dead into the glorious image of His firstborn? That will be the greatest miracle of all, and it won't come about by evolution!

Someday all our questions will be answered as the redeemed of the planet earth become witnesses to the destruction of the old universe and the creation of new heavens and a new earth. From our vantage point in the holy city, we will actually see the power of God at work. What a day of wonder and rejoicing that will be! God will need only to speak and it will all come to pass as God has promised:

> And all the host of heaven shall be dissolved, and the heavens shall be rolled together as a scroll: and all their host shall fall down.
>
> Isaiah 34:4

> For, behold, I create new heavens and a new earth: and the former shall not be remembered, nor come into mind.
>
> Isaiah 65:17

So then, who really cares how old the present earth is? It is a cursed planet, destined to be destroyed. We look forward with sublime anticipation to the grandeur of a new universe and a pristine planet where sin shall be no more. It is my point of view that the holy city, from which we will be eyewitnesses of the new creation, will settle down upon the new earth, where we will dwell with God forever!

And I saw a new heaven and a new earth: for the first heaven and the first earth were passed away; and there was no more sea. And I John saw the holy city, new Jerusalem, coming down from God out of heaven, prepared as a bride adorned for her husband.

Revelation 21: 1, 2

49
The Painting

I recall it was small,
And it hung on the wall
Obscure and apart from the rest.
In surroundings so bare
That few noticed it there;
The picture I loved as the best.

In so gay an array
Of fine paintings that day,
Indeed, not a soul would have guessed,
That a painting as plain
And apart could contain
A beauty none other possessed.

It had not a fine frame,
Nor the artist a name;
No outstanding colors beguiled.
Although faded I fear,
Still the features were clear
In the face of a little child.

I recall it was small,
And it hung in the hall,
Where I lingered for many a while;
Quite entranced by the grace,
For in that little face,
The artist had captured a smile.

Now often I ponder,
As memories wander,

The glorious scenes I'd construe.
Were I able to paint
All the beauty contained
In the kindnesses we do.

50

I Wish I Had Said That

Sanctify the Lord God in your hearts: and be ready always to give an answer to every man that asketh you a reason of the hope that is in you with meekness and fear.

1 Peter 3:15

Many times after we have heard a particularly witty remark or the perfect answer to a perturbable question, we say to ourselves, "I wish I had said that!" An opportunity to witness often occurs when we are asked the familiar question, "Are you Catholic or Protestant?" I hope next time I will say something like this. "I am a child of God, but not by being a member of a Catholic or a Protestant church, not by being baptized, nor by living a good moral life.

"I am a child of God because I have experienced a spiritual rebirth through faith in Jesus Christ and by God's grace! God's Holy Spirit now dwells in me, making me a supernatural being and a son in the family of God. I cannot classify myself as either a Catholic or a Protestant, because the Word of God tells me there is only one church. All those who have truly been born again are members of that one church, regardless of their earthly denomination. This is an indisputable fact clearly stated in the Holy Scriptures again and again. If you understand this and still want to know what I am, I suppose it is best summed up by the word *Christian.*"

The problem remains that there are many who call themselves Christian who don't really know how to be one. Almost all people believe in God, but their hearts are still troubled because they don't know His Son. Jesus said, "Let not your heart be troubled: ye believe in God, believe also in Me. . . . I am the way, the truth, and the life: no man cometh unto the Father, but by me" (John 14:1, 6).

These words from the Lord have the ring of eternity in them. They are sublimely simple but profoundly deep. Their surface meaning is clear enough for a little child to understand, yet the greatest theologians have not yet fully probed their depth!

Becoming a Christian involves a two-way covenant with God. He saves us and keeps us by our simple acceptance of Jesus Christ as our Savior; we in turn make Jesus Christ our Lord by our obedience. Jesus said, "Not every one that saith unto me, Lord, Lord, shall enter into the kingdom of heaven; but he that doeth the will of my Father which is in heaven" (Matthew 7:21).

Such a challenge is not answered by simply joining a religious denomination, not by church attendance, nor by doing "the best we can." It requires discipleship!

Someone has wisely said (and I wish I had said it first), "Without the Way, there is no going; without the Truth, there is no knowing; and without the Life, there is no growing." We need to know what Jesus meant when He said, "I am the way, the truth, and the life."

Christ Is the Way

Christ is more than *a* way of life; Christianity is more than a good way to live. Jesus Christ is *the* Way! There is no other way whereby mankind can be saved from death and eternal hell. Christ is the only answer to all the problems of mankind. Only He can give the peace that passeth all understanding. Not long ago a hard-bitten journalist for one of the largest newspaper syndicates in the world stated that Billy Graham has done more good in Europe and Great Britain in the space of a few short weeks than all our propaganda since the end of World War II. Not because he sold America or the American way of life, but because he faithfully presented Jesus Christ as the Way. The world is fed up with hearing about America, but it is starving for Jesus Christ!

When we are willing to accept Jesus in a simple childlike faith, and when we are willing to surrender our ways to the holy will of God, *then* Jesus is the Way whereby we become Christians.

Christ Is the Truth

Pilate asked the question, "What is truth?" with the very epitome of truth, the Lord Jesus Christ, standing there before him. *Jesus* is the Word of Truth incarnate. The blindness of Pilate forcefully exemplifies the blindness of a lost world. Our Lord Jesus said to the Father in His high priestly prayer, "thy word is truth" (John 17:17). The Apostle John wrote that the "Word was made flesh, and dwelt among us" (John 1:14). The Bible is the written Word of truth, and Jesus is the living Word of truth.

Religions that consist of manufactured doctrines contrary to the inspired Holy Scriptures are satanic. They are the antithesis of truth. Christ is not merely *a* truth, as all religions must confess. He is *the* truth, as God has confirmed again and again in His Word. Jesus said to His disciples, "ye shall know the truth, and the truth shall make you free" (John 8:32). The Apostle John has also written, "But whoso keepeth his word, in him verily is the love of God perfected" (1 John 2:5).

Christ Is the Life

Christ and Christ alone is the source of spiritual life. The Bible says simply, "He that hath the Son hath life; and he that hath not the Son of God hath not life" (1 John 5:12). Jesus said, "I am come that they might have life, and that they might have it more abundantly" (John 10:10). Without Christ we are physically alive but spiritually dead! The Bible clearly teaches that unless we receive new life through a spiritual rebirth, we are dead in trespasses and sins. "And you hath he quickened, who were dead in trespasses and sins" (Ephesians 2:1).

Yet there are those false teachers who by the inspiration of the devil proclaim that we are *all* God's children, thus denying the necessity of the new birth and the new life. They deny the existence of a literal hell, but God has said that the destiny of the "dead" is hell and ultimately the lake of fire. "And I saw the dead, small and great, stand before God. . . . and death and hell delivered up the dead which were in them. . . . And whosoever was not found written in the book of life was cast into the lake of fire" (Revelation 20:12, 13, 15).

Jesus Christ then is the *Way* to heaven, the *Truth* to the renewing of our minds, and *Life* eternal to all who are truly born again into the family of God. We are all members of one holy church, and we are all one in Him. As members of His body, we are all related by His precious blood. By His Spirit we are all "baptized into one body, whether we be Jews or Gentiles, whether we be bond or free" (1 Corinthians 12:13).

And so our Lord prayed for the unity of His church: "That they may all be one; as thou, Father, art in me, and I in thee, that they also may be one in us" (John 17:21).

Brethren, God is not pleased with our manmade divisions, our self-righteousness and religious convictions that divide brothers and sisters in Christ. He wants us to recognize and work for the unity of the body. Our business is not denominational, nor should we be involved in proselytizing men from one so-called faith to another. We are called to be witnesses to the Way, the Truth, and the Life. As the Apostle Paul wrote to the church at Corinth, "For I determined not to know any thing among you, save Jesus Christ, and him crucified" (1 Corinthians 2:2).

That is the message that convicts the unsaved. That simple message tells us how we become Christians—and I'm glad I said that!

51

The Race of Man

In a dream I saw them pass
In narrow never-ending line.
I saw each eye that hurried by,
But wavered not to look in mine.
All intent on things ahead,
Not content with those nearby,
I could not cause a soul to pause,
For of another world was I.

I beside them ran, but they
Were somehow strangely unaware.
A lonely ghost amid the host
Of surging souls around me there.
I might, I thought, discern at last
What lies beyond the eyes extreme.
The answers sought through ages past
Unveiled for me in a dream.

Along the road of life we sped,
Passed the sorrows, joys, and tears;
Passed the morrow, forged ahead,
Like minutes passed the fleeting years.
Faster, faster, time was master,
Waiting not for foolish men
Who wandered wide at each divide,
And humbly stumbled back again.

We climbed the mount of "Work to Do,"
We climbed to see the setting sun,
And from the summit gained the view,
The true reward of work well done.
We found the valley of romance,

The grace of nature made the scene,
The place enhanced where lovers danced,
And I, the Phantom, danced between.

The race went on, the pace was great.
My strength was not the same, I found,
My youth was gone, and oft of late,
I faltered on the rougher ground.
Around me those who led the way
Were ailing, and I wondered why.
Alas, had they grown old and gray?
Yes, some were older still than I.

There came the sound of rushing air.
The air we found was damp with rain.
We fought through thickets of despair,
And sought the open road again.
Then the sky grew dark, and fear
Crept through the trembling, stricken crowd.
Someone shrieked, "The end is here!"
"And this is death!" I cried aloud.

Smash! the heavens burst asunder!
Flashed the lightning on the hill!
Crashed the world beneath the thunder!
Came the end and all was still.
It was dawn, the night was gone.
The sun came streaming in on me.
O, had I not awakened then,
I might have seen *eternity!*

52
Strong Doctrine

Preach the word; be instant in season, out of season; reprove, rebuke, exhort with all longsuffering and doctrine. For the time will come when they will not endure sound doctrine; but after their own lusts shall they heap to themselves teachers, having itching ears; And they shall turn away their ears from the truth, and shall be turned unto fables.

2 Timothy 4:2-4

The season is fast approaching, and may in fact be already upon the Lord's church, when strong doctrine will no longer be endured. In America, where we still enjoy religious liberty, the real danger to the church is from within the church! Many denominations previously considered fundamental and evangelical are compromising the Holy Scriptures with contemporary, humanist philosophy. Most church pastors seem to be afraid of offending their lukewarm constituents. While urging Christian morality, they condemn not the rising tide of adultery, fornication, homosexuality, and abortion. They are vague on such issues as divorce, the role of women in the church, and the Lord's implicit instructions to both men and women in regard to family responsibilities. Very little mention is made any more regarding the fate of the lost. Whatever happened to hell? Neither are the redeemed being called to work out their salvation in fear and trembling. Much of organized religion seems primarily obsessed with self-perpetuation. The radio and television churches have a great zeal for more and more air time, not necessarily to reach the unsaved, but to promote their own moral and political beliefs. They have an insatiable need for money to support their many endeavors, and their appeals are bringing in millions of dollars. Their most enviable success in this respect is causing our governmental fathers to question the tax-exempt status the church has so long enjoyed!

The multiplicity of religious organizations inundating America includes a variety of cults our founding fathers would have refused to recognize. Meanwhile the truly Christian churches are not preaching the Gospel with convicting, old-time power. In fact the current rhetoric of the church is hardly distinguishable from the language of the cults. It seems predictable, therefore, that the courts of our land will no longer be able to define a false cult, but will eventually lump them all, along with the church, into the category of organized religion and deal with us all accordingly.

Brethren, the Supreme Court may not be able to separate a false cult from the true church, but God's people should know the difference. The Bible-believing churches of America had better return soon to preaching the sound doctrine of the apostles without apology! Otherwise, the spirit of antichrist will hasten our impending demise.

The Deity of Christ

Jesus said to His apostles:

Whom say ye that I am? And Simon Peter answered and said, Thou are the Christ, the Son of the living God. And Jesus answered and said unto him, Blessed art thou, Simon Barjona: for flesh and blood hath not revealed it unto thee, but my Father which is in heaven. And I say also unto thee, That thou are Peter [*Petros,* a little rock], and upon this rock [*Petra*] I will build my church; and the gates of hell shall not prevail against it.

Matthew 16:15-18

The Apostle John wrote, "Who is a liar but he that denieth that Jesus is the Christ? He is antichrist, that denieth the Father and the Son. Whosoever denieth the Son, the same hath not the Father" (1 John 2:22, 23).

The great central truth of the Holy Scriptures is that Jesus is the Rock, the Christ and Anointed One promised in the Old Testament. He and the Father are one. Jesus Christ is God made manifest in human flesh. He is Immanuel! The prophet Isaiah has written, "his name shall be called Wonderful, Counsellor, The mighty God, The everlasting Father, The Prince of Peace" (Isaiah 9:6). Isaiah also declared, "Look unto me, and be ye saved, all the ends of the earth; for I am God, and there is none else. . . . unto me every knee shall bow, every tongue shall swear [confess]" (Isaiah 45:22, 23).

The doctrine of the Lord's apostles is that Jesus is the great I AM of the Old Testament. The Apostle Paul, in regard to Isaiah's prophecy, has written, "That at the name of Jesus every knee should bow . . . And that every tongue should confess that Jesus Christ is Lord, to the glory of God the Father" (Philippians 2:10, 11).

Jesus was not just another great prophet. He was not just the great example that we should emulate, nor the pinnacle of human attainment. He was not an angel, or another god among many gods. Such doctrine is blasphemy, but it is the widely accepted doctrine of the cults! They deny that Jesus is God. They deny the truth of the Holy Trinity. They ridicule the reality of God the Father, God the Son, and God the Holy Spirit in one person. They deny the clear teaching of the Scriptures regarding the deity of Christ.

Fire and Brimstone

The doctrine of eternal hell and the power and person of Satan are subjects seldom heard in our churches anymore. We have gotten away from that old-fashioned "fire and brimstone" scary style of preaching. Most expositors refer only to a "Christless eternity" as the final destination of the lost. That doesn't sound so bad, does it? The unsaved can reason that they are getting along without Christ in this life, so why fear death? What is there to be saved from? Brethren, the Bible clearly teaches that all who will not accept Jesus Christ as the Savior in this life are going to eternal hell! And there is indeed a powerful satanic person, a real devil. He is the deceiver of the lost. Listen to these warnings from Holy Scripture.

And if thine eye offend thee, pluck it out: it is better for thee to enter into the kingdom of God with one eye, than having two eyes to be cast into hell fire: Where their worm dieth not, and the fire is not quenched.

Mark 9:47, 48

And the devil that deceived them was cast into the lake of fire and brimstone, where the beast and the false prophet are, and shall be tormented day and night for ever and ever.

... And I saw the dead, small and great, stand before God; and the books were opened. ... And whosoever was not found written in the book of life was cast into the lake of fire.

Revelation 20: 10, 12, 15

The reality of Satan and eternal hell is sound doctrine!

The Efficacy of the Lord's Blood

True religion is a "bloody" religion. Moses' wife, Zipporah, said, "A bloody husband thou art"(Exodus 4:26). And so we are a blood-sprinkled people. As the Word of God declares, "For the life of the flesh is in the blood: and I have given it to you upon the altar to make an atonement for your souls: for it is the blood that maketh an atonement for the soul" (Leviticus 17:11).

"And without shedding of blood is no remission" (Hebrews 9:22).

It was necessary for God to enter human life and to partake of a human body without the aid of a human father so that His resulting sinless blood could be the perfect atonement for sin forever. Though that blood flowed through human veins, it was not derived from Adam. It was the unique blood of the One who was and never ceased to be the second Person of the Godhead. This, brethren, is not popular theology. It is not often heard from the pulpits of our land anymore, but it is sound doctrine, for as the Apostle Peter has written, "Forasmuch as ye know that ye were not redeemed with corruptible things, as silver and gold ... But with the precious blood of Christ" (1 Peter 1:18, 19).

True Religion Is a Sexist Religion

Ours is also a sexist religion. After Adam and Eve had sinned, God said to Eve, and therefore to all women, "I will greatly multiply thy sorrow and thy conception; in sorrow thou shalt bring forth children; and thy desire shall be to thy husband, and he shall rule over thee" (Genesis 3:16).

God said to Adam, and therefore to all men, "Cursed is the ground for thy sake; in sorrow shalt thou eat of it all the days of thy life" (Genesis 3:17).

Job, in the agony of the Lord's testing, cried out: "Man that is born of a woman is of few days, and full of trouble. He cometh forth like a flower, and is cut down: he fleeth also as a shadow, and continueth not" (Job 14:1, 2).

But the good news of the Gospel is, as the Apostle John has written, "Whosoever [man or woman] believeth that Jesus is the Christ is born of God" (1 John 5:1).

Brethren, when we are born into the family of the triune God, He becomes our heavenly Father. We are saved from the curse and from hell by the finished work of His Son, and we (both male and female) are made temples for His Spirit to dwell in. We are called to participate in distinctive male and female roles for His glory. God has made Christ the head of the church and every man the head of his own family. And so the Apostle Paul has written, "For the husband is the head of the wife, even as Christ is the head of the church: and he is the saviour of the body. Therefore as the church is subject unto Christ, so let the wives be to their own husbands in every thing" (Ephesians 5:23, 24).

This too is sound doctrine.

True Religion Is not a Democracy

Our Christian bookstores are flooded with the commentaries of teachers who write for the edification of those with itching ears who can no longer endure sound doctrine. Many of these teachers have not been Christians for very long themselves, yet they have all the answers! The records of their successful, joyful, rewarding lives since being born again, coupled with their exciting experiences and special revelations from the Holy Spirit, are causing some of us older Christians to wonder how we missed out on all this. Much of what they say is true, of course, but it is my point of view that they are pouring out a steady diet of baby food, not the strong meat of the Gospel.

Meanwhile, our church councils are debating their doctrinal positions on such topics as the role of women in the church, premarital sex, divorce, abortion, homosexuality, creation versus evolution, and the inerrancy of the Holy Scriptures. Brethren, these are not topics to be voted upon! True religion is not a democracy. It is a theocracy! We must obey God if we would serve Him. We cannot repeal the Ten Commandments.

Sound Doctrine Begets Discipleship

Sound doctrine is not predicated upon emotions and experiences. Neither does the new birth guarantee success by this world's standards. We will still have tribulations after we are saved and for as long as we are yet in Adam's likeness. God never promised us a rose garden, not in this life! But He has promised that He will share our burdens and He will give us an inner joy and peace that this world knows nothing about. Jesus said: "These things I have spoken unto you, that in me ye might have peace. In the world ye shall have tribulation: but be of good cheer; I have overcome the world" (John 16:33).

We are exhorted to "desire the sincere milk of the word" while we are babes in Christ, "that ye may grow thereby" (1 Peter 2:2). But growing to spiritual maturity requires that we soon feed on the meat of the Word, that we might become the steadfast, unmovable Christians that God wants us to be. Sound doctrine is learned from the Bible as we study to show ourselves approved unto God (*see* 2 Timothy 2:15).

Sound doctrine is not popular; it demands continuing personal conviction, repentance, confession, self-sacrifice, and obedience. God's Holy Word, thoroughly masticated and digested, nourishes our spiritual bodies and gives us spiritual discernment. With our feet upon the Rock (Petra), we will not faint when trials come, we will not fall victim to false teaching and the cults. Sound doctrine, coupled with our desire to do the Father's holy will, will lead us in paths of righteousness for His name's sake. Sound doctrine begets discipleship!

53

Palm Sunday

Rejoice greatly, O daughter of Zion; shout, O daughter of Jerusalem: behold, thy King cometh unto thee: he is just, and having salvation; lowly, and riding upon an ass, and upon a colt the foal of an ass.

Zechariah 9:9

On Palm Sunday our thoughts are generally directed to our Lord's triumphal entry into Jerusalem. We are reminded how the multitudes spread palm branches in His path and cried, "Hosanna in the highest," as He rode past. But through it all, our Lord was sad, and when He came to Jerusalem, He wept over it. Brethren, it always grips my heart when I think of our omnipotent God weeping. Why must God weep? I think it is because there is one thing God cannot do: He cannot make us love Him! He could easily put us on our knees in fear and trembling. He could make us do His will, but He wants our love. He loves us so much that He became man, took our sins upon Himself, and died in our place! He wants us to experience His perfect love, for "perfect love casteth out fear" (1 John 4:18). He wept over Jerusalem, but He was weeping for all of Israel and for all men who will not accept His love.

The crowds who cheered Him that day felt their Messiah had come at last! They believed that Jesus would rule from the throne of His father, David. They hoped He would at last overthrow the yoke of Roman oppression and they would be free. Had not the temple been rebuilt and made ready? Was not this the Messiah riding on a colt as prophesied? Had not the voice of John the Baptist called out from the wilderness, "Prepare ye the way of the Lord"? Surely now all the prophecies regarding the restoration of Israel would be fulfilled and the glory of the Lord would shine upon her!

But later, when Jesus explained that His Kingdom was not of this world, when He told them that He must die, when He warned them of the trials that would come, and when they counted the cost of being His disciples, the multitudes deserted Him! Many of those who had shouted, "Hosanna in the highest," were soon shouting, "Away with Him! Crucify Him! We have no king but Caesar!"

What Israel wanted then, and what the world wants now, is a social gospel. They want a Messiah who will bring them freedom from all forms of oppression, freedom from want, freedom from problems, freedom from all restraints, and the freedom to do their own thing!

Brethren, that's why the false cults are so successful in attracting adherents. The messiahs of the cults promise heaven on earth. They tell people what they want to hear. They make promises they can never keep. And in the last days the most successful of them all will be the "whore that sitteth upon many waters," the apostate church of the antichrist described in the Book of Revelation (17:1).

Our Lord never promised the church that serving Him would be easy. He never promised to make us rich and successful (not by this world's standards). He never promised us that we would never be overcome by illness or that we would never know troubles and discouragement. He said, "In the world ye shall have tribulation: but be of good cheer; I have overcome the world" (John 16:33).

The true church recognizes that this world is not our home; we look for a city that will be greater than any of the kingdoms of this world shall ever be! We look for the coming again of our Messiah as King of Kings and Lord of Lords. We have a peace of heart and mind that this world knows nothing of, because we are in Him and He is in us. Our joy is in serving Him now, in spite of our trials. We know that whatever He allows is for our ultimate good and that He is making us ready for the greater life yet to come.

Our attitude at this joyous season, I believe, should not be unlike that of our Lord's on that first Palm Sunday. We are saddened by the superficial joy and hosannas of the multitudes who celebrate but do not really know our Lord and will soon fall away when trials come. We need to weep for the lost. Our hearts should be broken for the unsaved. But we also have that inward peace and joy that comes to all who are truly born again, because we know the Messiah as our Savior and Lord! And we have a hope that cannot be shaken.

Wherein ye greatly rejoice, though now for a season, if need be, ye are in heaviness through manifold temptations: That the trial of your faith, being much more precious than of gold that perisheth, though it be tried with fire, might be found unto praise and honour and glory at the appearing of Jesus Christ: Whom having not seen, ye love; in whom, though now ye see him not, yet believing, ye rejoice with joy unspeakable and full of glory.

1 Peter 1:6-8

54

The Signs of the Spirit

Now if any man have not the Spirit of Christ, he is none of his.

Romans 8:9

Membership in the early apostolic church required evidence of the presence of the Holy Spirit in the life of the believer. When believers were later appointed to positions of responsibility and authority such as deacon, elder, or missionary, the church looked for those who were filled with the Spirit. The Holy Spirit is the sign that we have indeed been born again into the family of God. "The Spirit itself beareth witness with our spirit, that we are the children of God" (Romans 8:16).

If the Holy Spirit of God dwells in us, we know it, and the fruit of the Spirit in our lives is evident to others who know us. *We cannot be secret Christians.* If we have not the Spirit of God, we are not Christians at all.

When we were born again, it was by the Spirit. In the process of conversion, it is the Holy Spirit who first calls and convicts us of our sins and our need to repent and be saved. "And when he [the Holy Spirit] is come, he will reprove [convict] the world of sin, and of righteousness, and of judgment" (John 16:8).

When we accept Jesus Christ as our Savior, we are born again by the Holy Spirit. "Except a man be born of water and of the Spirit, he cannot enter into the kingdom of God" (John 3:5).

We are baptized into the body of Christ by the Holy Spirit. "For by one Spirit are we all baptized into one body" (1 Corinthians 12:13).

And the Holy Spirit takes up residence in our mortal bodies. "What? know ye not that your body is the temple of the Holy Ghost which is in you, which ye have of God, and ye are not your own?" (1 Corinthians 6:19).

All born again believers, whether they are newborn babes in Christ or mature Christians, have the Holy Spirit of God within them. He is there to guide and direct our lives and to help us grow more and more Christlike. We need to pray always that the Holy Spirit might have His way. When we are yielded to Him, we are in the center of God's holy will.

However, Christians can resist the Spirit, grieve the Spirit, and quench the Spirit. When we do, we cannot remain in God's will. We are out of fellowship, and He cannot bless our daily lives. We become miserable. This is one of the signs of the Spirit, one of the ways we can know that we are the children of God: We can no longer enjoy sin.

Conversely, we find that our greatest joy comes from being obedient to God. When we so live that we glorify Him, we find fulfillment and blessing and peace. It requires our yielding to the Holy Spirit within us. It requires keeping our bodies under control and making them fit and clean vessels, prepared for the Master's use.

We should begin each new day with the prayer that God will fill us with His Spirit, lead us by His Spirit, and make us a blessing to all whose lives we touch. This requires self-denial on our part. It requires putting to death the sins of the flesh that make us unfit vessels and discredit our testimony. "And they that are Christ's have crucified the flesh with the affections and lusts" (Galatians 5:24).

What then are the signs of the Spirit-filled Christian? I believe that primarily they are what the Apostle Paul has designated the fruit of the Spirit. "But the fruit of the Spirit is love, joy, peace, longsuffering, gentleness, goodness, faith, meekness, temperance: against such there is no law" (Galatians 5:22, 23).

Note that these are not "fruits" of the Spirit but "fruit" (singular). You cannot possess one or two of these attributes of Jesus Christ and not the others if you are filled with the Holy Spirit. It is by His fruit that the world sees Jesus in us. These qualities are the true signs of the Spirit. The fruit of the Spirit should not be confused with the gifts of the Spirit. There is a spirit of error abroad in the church today that teaches that gifts are the true signs of the Spirit. God has given particular gifts to His people, but they were never meant to be enduring signs. As the Apostle Paul has written:

For to one is given by the Spirit the word of wisdom; to another the word of knowledge by the same Spirit; To another faith by the same Spirit; to another the gifts of healing by the same Spirit; To another the working of miracles; to another prophecy; to another discerning of spirits; to another divers kinds of tongues; to another the interpretation of tongues.

1 Corinthians 12:8-10

These gifts of the Spirit are provided as helps to our Christian work and witness, but they can all be duplicated by Satan and his followers. They are not dependable signs. Remember how the magicians of Pharaoh could duplicate the miracles of Moses and Aaron? Our Lord Jesus spoke of some who cast out demons in His name as being workers of iniquity (*see* Matthew 7:22, 23). And in the last days we are told how the antichrist will do great wonders "and deceiveth them that dwell on the earth by the means of those miracles which he had power to do" (Revelation 13:14).

Again, my brethren, the true signs of the Spirit are those likenesses of Jesus Christ that are seen in the Spirit-filled Christian. By them we know that Christ is living in us. The Holy Spirit of God gives us a desire to be holy, as He is holy. He gives us a concern for the unsaved. He gives us a love for His Word. He makes us want to spend more time in prayer. He gives us a concern regarding the way we spend our time. He makes us want to do our Father's will. By His urging we seek to glorify our Father in heaven. The unsaved have no such concerns. Jesus said, "Let your light so shine before men, that they may see your good works, and glorify your Father which is in heaven" (Matthew 5:16).

When our heart's desire is to obey this commandment, it is the surest sign of all that the Holy Spirit of God is in control and that the fruit of the Spirit will indeed be seen in us in all that we say and do.

55
Who Is the Victor?

The purpose of a sport or game,
As games were first intended,
Today somehow is not the same,
The object not so splendid.

We need to have some kind of fun
Offsetting daily care,
We need to walk and jump and run,
Who toil from a chair.

We need to laugh and sing aloud,
We need fresh air and flowers,
We need to mingle with the crowd,
We need some carefree hours.

But in our sports and games today,
The emphasis, it seems,
Is not so much on being gay,
But more on having winning teams.

Some seem to think it somehow sin
To lose or fall a little short,
A team that doesn't usually win,
Deserves not our support.

Some men are really sore and cross
As the game comes to an end,
They seem to think the day a loss
When losing to a friend.

Who is the real victor then?
Who stands to gain the more?
To me it's the fellow having fun
Regardless of the score.

56

Time

Our Part of the Mystery

To every thing there is a season, and a time to every purpose under the heaven.

Ecclesiastes 3:1

As finite human beings, we are bound by the dimension of time. Only God is infinite and eternal; we cannot even comprehend such an existence! Everything that we are capable of understanding must have a beginning and an end, but God is the great I AM, the eternally existent One. In His heavenly abode, He enjoys His eternal works. Surrounded by angelic beings He created and who shall never grow old, He looks down on the universe in which we humans dwell, and His omniscient mind knows the past, the present, and the future, which we understand and experience only as time allows.

Time began, I suppose, when God created the heavens and the earth. Therefore, the Holy Spirit has dictated in the Scriptures, "In the beginning God created the heaven and the earth" (Genesis 1:1). The universe in which we live had a beginning, and God knew from the beginning that this present, particular universe must also have an end. God knew what sin would do, and He knew what He must do to defeat sin forever. Someday He will create a new heaven and a new earth, where there will be no more time. Like heaven, the present abode of God, it will be an eternal universe prepared for a new creation, a finished work of mankind not only made in the image and likeness of God, but also glorified! Here God will take up His new abode with His children and dwell with them forever. Even now He is preparing certain eternal dwelling places (mansions) for those who are trusting His Son for salvation.

Meanwhile, God is dealing with sinful mankind and with Satan, our tempter, in the time He has foreknown and allowed. He has a timetable for all His works, and He must wait until all things have been fulfilled. His Holy Spirit revealed to His ancient prophets all those things which must come to pass, and we who are Christ's have seen the fulfillment of every promise up until the calling out of His church (the rapture). Much of His future planning has to do with His chosen people, Israel, who must yet come to repentance. All of the events in the life of this nation, past, present, and future—their glorious triumphs and bitter defeats—were known and written of before by the inspiration of the Holy Spirit. We Gentiles can only look on in awe as we see how God is working out through them His complete plan for all mankind. Through them, indeed, will all the nations of the earth be blessed, first, by the unspeakable gift of the Savior: "But when the fulness of the time was come, God sent forth his Son, made of a woman, made under the law, To redeem them that were under the law, that we might receive the adoption of sons" (Galatians 4:4, 5).

Second, Jesus is coming again! This time He will come with a shout and we who are looking and longing for His coming will be caught up to meet Him in the air. As far as we can tell from the Holy Scriptures, all prophecy prior to this glorious event has been fulfilled, and He could call out His saints at any moment. No one knows the time of this event—not even the angels—but God knows. It was known and planned by Him from the beginning.

As we watch for His blessed appearance, we are admonished to redeem the time we have left, to use it boldly to proclaim the Gospel and make it count for His glory. We shall have to give account for the way we have used the time allowed us after we were saved. "Walk in wisdom toward them that are without, redeeming the time. Let your speech be alway with grace, seasoned with salt, that ye may know how ye ought to answer every man" (Colossians 4:5, 6).

I know that as I grow older, I am more and more concerned about time. I want to be involved in works that have eternal value. I want to see all my family saved and growing in the Lord. I want to be the kind of husband, father, and grandfather that God wants me to be. I want to be a good witness to the unsaved and a blessing to all who know me. I want to be a clean and usable vessel, fit for the work of His Holy Spirit.

Following the rapture, I believe there will be a time of great tribulation upon the earth when God will pour out His wrath on those who will not repent. The Bible teaches it will be a period of seven years. During the last half of this period will be the time of

Jacob's trouble. During this great affliction, Israel will at last come to repentance and Jesus will come again to destroy the armies of the world and save a remnant of His chosen people. The time of great tribulation will culminate in the battle of Armageddon.

Then our Lord will reign over all the world for a thousand years. Satan will be bound, and the planet earth will find her sabbath rest at last. During this time Israel will experience her greatest glory. Israel will at last become God's great witness to all the nations of the world, proclaiming that Jesus Christ was not only their Messiah and the Savior of all who will trust in Him, but also that Jesus is the Lord God, the great I AM who first revealed Himself to Moses. Israel will finally fulfill her predestined role to proclaim the truths of the Word of God. And as God has promised, Israel will bring forth fruit and her seed shall be as the sand of the sea.

But when the thousand years are finished, God will loose Satan for a little while, and he will deceive the unbelievers again. This will bring about the time of the end. God will destroy the last of this world's armies. He will judge all the unsaved from the beginning of time. He will cast them all into the lake of fire with Satan, their prince. He will utterly destroy the earth and this present universe. The Apostle Peter has written that they shall all "be dissolved, and the elements shall melt with fervent heat" (2 Peter 3:12).

"Nevertheless we, according to his promise, look for new heavens and a new earth, wherein dwelleth righteousness" (2 Peter 3:13).

God created the dimension of time for a very necessary but limited purpose. It will last only until Satan and sin are defeated and destroyed forever. Then time will be no more, and "I shall dwell in the house of the Lord forever" (Psalms 23:6).

> And I saw a new heaven and a new earth: for the first heaven and the first earth were passed away; and there was no more sea. And I John saw the holy city, new Jerusalem, coming down from God out of heaven, prepared as a bride adorned for her husband. And I heard a great voice out of heaven saying, Behold, the tabernacle of God is with men, and he will dwell with them, and they shall be his people, and God himself shall be with them, and be their God.
>
> Revelation 21:1-3

57

What Is a Cult?

*Because strait is the gate, and narrow is the way, which leadeth
unto life, and few there be that find it.*

Matthew 7:14

Webster's dictionary merely states that a cult is "A system of
religious worship or ritual." I believe we Christians need to know
the distinct difference between a so-called Christian cult and true
Christianity. There are many religions that in no way try to identify
themselves as Christian, *but there are cults that claim to be Christian,
and therein lies the danger!* Millions of sincere, honest seekers of
truth are being misled by their false teaching. Millions who have
been led to believe they are saved and on their way to heaven are
still lost and bound for eternity in hell! This is confirmed in the Word
of God.

Many will say to me in that day, Lord, Lord, have we not
prophesied in thy name? and in thy name have we cast out
devils? and in thy name done many wonderful works? And
then will I profess unto them, I never knew you: depart from
me, ye that work iniquity.

Matthew 7:22, 23

Many have been misled regarding their salvation. Many professing Christians have never really been born again into the family of
God; hence, the Lord does not know them. Adherents of the
so-called Christian cults face the same fate, because these cults deny
the basic Christian doctrines. There are many differences in belief
among the various cults, but there are two denials of fundamental
truth that are common to all of them: *They deny the reality of the
Trinity, and they deny the deity of Jesus Christ.* These are the primary
identification marks of a false religion or cult. We need not waste
time investigating them further.

When Jesus asked the disciples, "Whom do men say that I the Son of man am?" (Matthew 16:13), He was asking the key question that separates unbelievers from His true followers. The unconverted would say that He was perhaps John the Baptist, raised from the dead; or Elijah, the prophet; or Jeremiah. But when He asked the disciples, "But whom say ye that I am?" (Matthew 16:15), Peter replied, "Thou art the Christ, the Son of the living God" (Matthew 16:16). Jesus then stated that this is the truth upon which He would build His church. The cults are those who deny the Lord's own affirmation of His deity.

> Who is a liar but he that denieth that Jesus is the Christ? He is antichrist, that denieth the Father and the Son.
>
> 1 John 2:22

> Hereby know ye the Spirit of God: Every spirit that confesseth that Jesus Christ is come in the flesh is of God: And every spirit that confesseth not that Jesus Christ is come in the flesh is not of God: and this is that spirit of antichrist, whereof ye have heard that it should come; and even now already is it in the world.
>
> 1 John 4:2, 3

> This is he that came by water and blood, even Jesus Christ; not by water only, but by water and blood. And it is the Spirit that beareth witness, because the Spirit is truth. For there are three that bear record in heaven, the Father, the Word, and the Holy Ghost: and these three are one.
>
> 1 John 5:6, 7

The Bible clearly teaches that God is a Trinity. The Father, the Son, and the Holy Spirit are a union of three divine persons in one Godhead. It has always helped me to understand this when I realize that we, who were originally made in the image and likeness of God, are also a trinity. We are composed of a body, a soul, and a spirit, and yet we are one. When we die, the spirit and the soul leave the body and, fully conscious, await for the resurrection of the body. Our eternal destiny in either heaven or the lake of fire will be experienced by each of us as a trinity of body, soul, and spirit. This is sound doctrine. Therefore, any religion or cult that denies the

Trinity of God must also deny the trinity of man, a denial of the clear teaching of the Holy Scriptures.

Again, any religion that denies the deity of Christ—that is, that Jesus is God Himself—is a false religion or a cult. Many of these so-called Christian religions or cults recognize Jesus as a prophet, as a mighty angel, or even as another god, but they deny that He is the only eternal God. They deny this most important truth in the Bible. And they have blasphemed His holy name. In addition, they claim miraculous revelations beyond that which is written in the Scriptures, and they have added to the Scriptures their own books of false teaching. They have dared to teach their own interpretations of the Bible in spite of the clear warnings from Jesus in the very last book of the Bible.

> For I testify unto every man that heareth the words of the prophecy of this book, If any man shall add unto these things, God shall add unto him the plagues that are written in this book: And if any man shall take away from the words of the book of this prophesy, God shall take away his part out of the book (tree) of life, and out of the holy city, and from the things which are written in this book.
>
> Revelation 22:18, 19

Brethren, the denial of the reality of the Trinity of God and the denial of the truth that Jesus is God's revelation of Himself are the basic and distinct differences between a cult and true Christianity. These denials by the cults defy the authority of the Word of God! The following Holy Scriptures make it crystal clear that the LORD God of the Old Testament is the "Word . . . made flesh, and dwelt among us" (John 1:14).

> In the beginning God [Elohim] created the heaven and the earth.
>
> Genesis 1:1

> In the beginning was the Word [Jesus], and the Word was with God, and the Word was God.
>
> John 1:1

He [Jesus] was in the world, and the world was made by him, and the world knew him not.

John 1:10

Therefore the Lord himself shall give you a sign; Behold, a virgin shall conceive, and bear a son, and shall call his name Immanuel [God with us].

Isaiah 7:14

For unto us a child is born, unto us a son is given: and the government shall be upon his shoulder: and his name shall be called Wonderful, Counsellor, The mighty God, The everlasting Father, The Prince of Peace.

Isaiah 9:6

Tell ye, and bring them near; yea, let them take counsel together: who hath declared this from ancient time? ... have not I the Lord? and there is no God else beside me; a just God and a Saviour; there is none beside me. Look unto me, and be ye saved, all the ends of the earth: for I am God, and there is none else. I have sworn by myself, the word is gone out of my mouth in righteousness, and shall not return, That unto me every knee shall bow, every tongue shall swear [confess].

Isaiah 45:21-23

Wherefore God also hath highly exalted him, and given him a name which is above every name: That at the name of Jesus every knee should bow, of things in heaven, and things in earth, and things under the earth; And that every tongue should confess that Jesus Christ is Lord, to the glory of God the Father.

Philippians 2:9-11

For it pleased the Father than in him [Jesus] should all fulness dwell [all the fullness of the Godhead].

Colossians 1:19

Ye call me [Jesus] Master and Lord: and ye say well; for so I am.

John 13:13

Philip saith unto him, Lord, shew us the Father, and it sufficeth us. Jesus saith unto him, Have I been so long time with you, and yet hast thou not known me, Philip? he that hath seen me hath seen the Father.

John 14:8, 9

I and my Father are one.

John 10:30

And so God became man and dwelt among us, that we might know Him, whom to know is life eternal, and that He by the sacrifice of Himself might take away our sin. He died in our place and rose again. He ascended to heaven, from whence He will come again and receive us unto Himself. Meanwhile, His Spirit (the third person in the Trinity) dwells in the body of every born again believer. "I will not leave you comfortless: I will come to you" (John 14:18).

"At that day ye shall know that I am in my Father, and ye in me, and I in you" (John 14:20).

The apostles declared:

Know ye not that ye are the temple of God, and that the Spirit of God dwelleth in you?

1 Corinthians 3:16

Now if any man have not the Spirit of Christ, he is none of his.

Romans 8:9

But if our gospel be hid, it is hid to them that are lost: In whom the god of this world hath blinded the minds of them which believe not, lest the light of the glorious gospel of Christ, who is the image of God, should shine unto them. For we preach not ourselves, but Christ Jesus the Lord.

2 Corinthians 4:3-5

And he [Jesus] hath on his vesture and on his thigh a name
written, KING OF KINGS, AND LORD OF LORDS.
                                                        Revelation 19:16

Truly Christ is God, and there is none other. We could go on
and on citing Scripture after Scripture that confirms that Jesus is
the great I AM of the Old Testament. He declared it to His disciples.
Doubting Thomas confirmed it when, after seeing the nail prints in
His hands, he cried, "My Lord and my God" (John 20:28). Brethren,
no truly honest student of the Scriptures could come to any other
conclusion. Jesus is God, and when we get to heaven, we shall see
only one Person: We shall see the LORD in all His glory. We shall
see Jesus as He really is!

58
What Is Apostasy?

There are three enemies of the Lord's church, and Satan uses them all in his relentless attack. These enemies are atheism, the cults, and apostasy.

The most unsuccessful of this unholy trio is atheism. Even Satan must admit that man, originally created in the image and likeness of God, has an inherent and intuitive knowledge of his Creator. The most primitive of men in the remotest reaches of the earth have an awareness of a supreme power in the universe. They must, therefore, be taught to become atheists! Satan knows the folly of such persuasion, because it has never been very successful. Even in the beginning, Satan did not attempt to convince Eve that there was no God. He found it much easier to cause her to doubt the truth of the Word of God.

Subsequently, Satan has made false religion his most successful weapon. Mankind wants and needs to believe in a god of some kind, so the prince of darkness (Satan) deludes his followers by his cunning in preventing their coming to the light. He endorses any cult that denies the Gospel of Jesus Christ. These false cults are the enemy from without, that is, from outside the true church. The cults deny the reality of the Holy Trinity and the essential Christian doctrine that Jesus Christ was God's revelation of Himself! The cults all believe in God, but they follow prophets who never knew our Lord. They consider Jesus just another of the prophets or an angel or perhaps a secondary god. Satan enthusiastically endorses all such religions, and they are leading millions to eternity in the lake of fire!

However, although the people of the many different religions of the world have always outnumbered the people of God, the greatest danger to the Lord's church is not from without. It is from within! It is apostasy. Apostasy is the abandonment of the basic doctrines of the church. In the Book of Revelation we learn of the seventh church, the church of Laodicea, the lukewarm church that the Lord will spew out of His mouth! (*See* Revelation 3:16.) I believe this will be the condition of the church at the end of the church age. The seventh church will be a church with no effective testimony for Jesus Christ. It will continue to call itself a church even after our Lord has called out the true church to meet Him in the air. I believe that this apostate church will continue into the time of the great tribulation. Eventually, this church will worship the unholy trinity of Satan, the beast, and the false prophet. It will degenerate morally to become the great whore described in Revelation 17. The beast will endorse and use this church for a while, and Satan will give them power to deceive the world.

"And the woman was arrayed in purple and scarlet colour, and decked with gold and precious stones and pearls, having a golden cup in her hand full of abominations and filthiness of her fornication" (Revelation 17:4).

However, the beast will soon tire of this apostate vermin, and when he has no further use for her, he and the remaining ten great nations among the kingdoms of this world will literally destroy her from the face of the earth. There will be no more church of any kind near the end of the great tribulation.

"And the ten horns which thou sawest upon the beast, these shall hate the whore, and shall make her desolate and naked, and shall eat her flesh, and burn her with fire" (Revelation 17:16).

But the danger to the true and holy church is now. The apostate teachers among us now are already weakening the citadels of truth! The basic doctrines which the early church held most dear are being attacked from within our own ranks! I believe that the very heart of this cancer is the current ecumenical endeavor to unite us all under one banner. Unity is the cry. "Did not our Lord pray for the unity of the body of Christ?" is the persuasive question. To which we must all confess, "Yes, but not at the cost of the abandonment of sound doctrine, not at the cost of immoral permissiveness, not at the cost of compromise with the enemy, and not at the cost of becoming a powerless, useless church!" The Apostle Paul has clearly warned us of the danger:

> This know also, that in the last days perilous times shall come. For men shall be lovers of their own selves, covetous, boasters, proud, blasphemers, disobedient to parents, unthankful, unholy, Without natural affection, trucebreakers, false accusers, incontinent, fierce, despisers of those that

are good, Traitors, heady, highminded, lovers of pleasures
more than lovers of God; Having a form of godliness, but
denying the power thereof.

2 Timothy 3:1-5

Apostasy began very early in man's history. In the Epistle of
Jude we are warned of ungodly men who would turn "the grace of
our God into lasciviousness, and denying the only Lord God, and
our Lord Jesus Christ" (Jude 4).

"Woe unto them! for they have gone in the way of Cain, and ran
greedily after the error of Balaam for reward, and perished in the
gainsaying of Core" (Jude 11).

Cain, the first son of Adam and Eve, believed in God, but he
was disobedient, unthankful, and unholy. His way was to do what he
thought was right. He reasoned within himself that the fruit of the
ground, which he had labored to harvest, was sacrifice enough,
refusing to bring the sin offering that God had designated. He saw
no need for the shedding of blood. There are many in the church
today who agree. The apostate teachers in the ecumenical movement are endeavoring to remove all mention of the shed blood of
Jesus Christ from our theology. But the Word of God clearly states:
"And almost all things are by the law purged with blood, and without
shedding of blood is no remission" (Hebrews 9:22).

"Forasmuch as ye know that ye were not redeemed with corruptible things . . . But with the precious blood of Christ, as of a lamb
without blemish and without spot" (1 Peter 1:18, 19).

The way of the apostate, then, is to do that which is "right in his
own eyes" (Judges 21:25). The apostate church will deny the basic
doctrines of the Christian church. They will provide a powerless
religion that is more palatable to the masses.

The error of the Old Testament prophet Balaam was a religion
of self-advantage and personal glory. He was a prophet for hire. The
Apostle Peter wrote of him that he "loved the wages of unrighteousness" (2 Peter 2:15). Balaam was self-righteous, quick to perceive
the faults of others, and blind to his own iniquities. After viewing
the sins of Israel, he assumed that a righteous God must curse them.
He was blind to the doctrine of justification by faith. When he
learned that God would not curse those whom He had chosen,
Balaam sought to corrupt them further. He enticed them to commit

whoredom with the daughters of Moab and to bow down to their gods (*see* Numbers 25:1, 2; 31:16).

Similarly, the apostate teachers of today would have us believe that faith in Christ will insure success by this world's standards. Their credo states that all you must do is "believe" to attain popularity, health, and material wealth. Meanwhile they espouse no need for holy living. They wink at the immorality of our age and condemn not the sins of fornication, adultery, homosexuality, abortion, drugs, and the current all-prevailing lust for worldly pleasures. Brethren, the unrighteousness of professing Christians is destroying the witness of the Lord's church!

It is true that God cannot curse the truly saved, but He cannot condone sin. He will deal with those who are crucifying the Lord afresh! The error of Balaam is the error of the apostate church today, which would cover its own sins with a facade of social concerns. Hence the current pretense of brotherly love in matters of race, equal rights, discrimination, and world peace. These are admirable goals, but they are not attainable by demonstration, oration, or legislation! For God has said: "If my people, which are called by my name, shall humble themselves, and pray, and seek my face, and turn from their wicked ways; then will I hear from heaven, and will forgive their sin, and will heal their land" (2 Chronicles 7:14).

The third type of apostasy is exemplified by the "gainsaying of Korah" (Numbers 16). Fifteen hundred years before the birth of Christ, Korah and other men of the tribes of Israel challenged the authority of Moses and the priesthood of Aaron. They reasoned that all members of a holy congregation should have equal authority and that Moses and Aaron had no right to lift themselves up above the congregation of the Lord. What they were really challenging was the authority of the Word of God. (*Gainsaying* is speaking against the Word.) "And no man taketh this honour unto himself, but he that is called of God, as was Aaron" (Hebrews 5:4).

At that time in Israel's history, God had declared Aaron to be high priest as well as spokesman for Moses. The many other priests who served in the tabernacle and later in the temple were to come only from the tribe of Levi. Since the death and resurrection of our Lord Jesus Christ, we are instructed in the Word of God that there is no more need for the Levitical priesthood and that Christ Himself is now our high priest, interceding for us in heaven (Hebrews 6:20). We need no other mediator!

Yet there are those today in the congregation of the Lord who, like Korah, would usurp the high priesthood of Jesus Christ and deny the authority of His Holy Word. The Scriptures tell us that the veil before the Holy of Holies, into which only the high priest could go, was rent from the top to the bottom when Jesus died. But it was the will of men to mend the veil and continue a priesthood of imperfect intercessors. The earth opened up and swallowed Korah and his followers before they could pollute the children of Israel with their false teaching. And so God has also warned the church to beware of all false teaching, for again the danger is from within the holy congregation.

"But there were false prophets also among the people, even as there shall be false teachers among you, who privily shall bring in damnable heresies, even denying the Lord that bought them, and bring upon themselves swift destruction" (2 Peter 2:1).

Brethren, we have the complete and entire Word of God. The Holy Scriptures are our authority for Christian living. We need not be deceived by false teachers. *Apostasy, in a nutshell, is false teaching within the church!* The problem in many of the lukewarm and liberal churches of today is that so many of God's people would rather listen to clever, popular personalities than study for themselves. They love to hear what they want to hear. The natural man wants an easy religion, one that will not prick his conscience or prescribe a cross to bear. We are exposed to more "religious" thought and are reading more religious books than ever before in our history, but we are neglecting our study of the Word of God. The church of Jesus Christ today needs to turn again to the practice of Bible reading. We need teachers and preachers who are unafraid and unashamed to preach the Word.

Preach the word; be instant in season, out of season; reprove, rebuke, exhort with all longsuffering and doctrine. For the time will come when they will not endure sound doctrine; but after their own lusts shall they heap to themselves teachers, having itching ears; And they shall turn away their ears from the truth, and shall be turned unto fables.

2 Timothy 4:2-4

59

In the Beginning

In the beginning God created the heaven and the earth.
Genesis 1:1

The first verse in God's Holy Word is to me an exciting and informative prelude to all the wonderful revelations that follow. Unfortunately, it is too often merely read without comprehension or meditation regarding all that it is intended to relate.

Genesis 1:1 is more than a simple statement of fact. It deserves reading again. It requires the understanding of some essential truths not clearly revealed in the English translation. Because it is the first expression of the whole of all truth as given to us by God in His infallible Word, it should be studied fully and expectantly.

Disappointingly, most of the thought given to this verse and most of the commentaries written about it center only on the theme of when the beginning took place. Many earnest Bible scholars, on the basis of biblical chronology, insist on a very young earth, one that is approximately six thousand years old. Others, influenced by modern scientific thought, geological studies, astronomy, and carbon testing of fossils, are just as adamant that the heavens and the earth are millions of years old. The truth of the matter is that we cannot prove either theory by the Bible. The Bible doesn't tell us how long the earth was in existence before the creation of our ancestor, Adam. There very well could have been millions of years involved. We are told very little about our pristine planet, what it was like, and who may have originally inhabited it.

The "beginning" referred to in Genesis 1:1 is in reference to the earth and the heavens that we presently know and observe. God, however, is eternal; He had no beginning. It is mind-boggling, but we have to ask, and not irreverently, what God was doing before He created these heavens and this earth. We know nothing of the third heaven, the dwelling place of God (*see* 2 Corinthians 12:1-4). We know nothing of other of His creative works. We do know that He created angels, and that prior to the creation of Adam, they served Him. We know also that some of them "kept not their first estate, but left their own habitation" (Jude 6) and one angel in particular, called Lucifer and Satan, ruled in a place called Eden (Ezekiel 28:13) quite unlike the Eden that Adam knew. We know that Satan had sinned against God and that he was waiting here on planet earth to tempt God's new creation.

The prophet Jeremiah seems to make reference to the second verse in the Bible, and his revelation is that a judgment from God had taken place. Note the following comparison of Scriptures.

"And the earth was without form, and void; and darkness was upon the face of the deep" (Genesis 1:2).

It is noteworthy that the Hebrew word for *was* can just as correctly be translated "became." This would allow the possibility that the earth that God created in the beginning became without form and void. This would correspond with Jeremiah's account of a judgment from God upon the earth and upon certain of its inhabitants.

> I beheld the earth, and, lo, it was without form, and void; and the heavens, and they had no light. I beheld the mountains, and, lo, they trembled, and all the hills moved lightly. I beheld, and, lo, there was no man, and the birds of the heaven were fled. I beheld, and, lo, the fruitful place was a wilderness, and all the cities thereof were broken down at the presence of the Lord, and by his fierce anger.
> Jeremiah 4:23-26

We need, too, to note the following from Isaiah: "Behold, the Lord maketh the earth empty, and maketh it waste, and turneth it upside down, and scattereth abroad the inhabitants thereof" (Isaiah 24:1).

When did these things occur? It is apparently not a picture of the Noahic flood, when eight people and two of every type of birds and animals were spared. This is a scene of utter devastation, with no survivors. It doesn't compare with the description of the end of the world, when, as we read in the New Testament, "the heavens shall pass away with a great noise, and the elements shall melt with fervent heat, the earth also and the works that are therein shall be burned up" (2 Peter 3:10).

The verses from Jeremiah and Isaiah could very well describe a judgment from God on a pre-Adamite creation. They could be a prelude to a new beginning, when God would make men in His own image and likeness. God's fierce anger in turning the earth upside down could account for the ice age and the destruction of prehistoric mammals and other creatures Adam never knew!

The "first day" referred to in Genesis 1:5 was when God caused light to shine upon the earth after the great darkness. No creative act is implied. It could have been that the sun and the stars had merely been hid for a time. Consider the following verse: "And God made two great lights; the greater light to rule the day, and the lesser light to rule the night: he made the stars also" (Genesis 1:16).

The word *made* is from the Hebrew *asah*, which is declarative of the fact that God brought the sun, the moon, and the stars into existence and is supportive of their intended purpose. Again, the verse does not say that God *created* them on the first day. In fact, there are no creative acts described in any of the first four days of Genesis 1. What occurred during these first four days could have been, as many Bible scholars, believe, a process of recreation of our planet preparatory to the creation of new life!

We just don't really know when God originally created the heavens and the earth. It is my point of view that we shall never know in this life. The Bible was written for the descendants of Adam, and it is foolish to argue the works of God prior to Adam.

More importantly, we should try to understand fully the things that the Word of God does make amply clear and that were intended for our edification. Returning our thoughts to Genesis 1:1, we should know that the first word for God in the Bible is from the Hebrew *Elohim.* "In the beginning [Elohim] created the heaven and the earth."

Elohim is a strange, wonderful, and awe-inspiring name for God. It implies power and strength. From it we see God as the Cause of creation. It denotes God as a person, specifically the Strong One. He is the true origin of force or energy and the Creator of matter. Further, Elohim is a uni-plural noun comprehending the Trinity of Father, Son, and Holy Spirit in one person. Thus the Scriptures are grammatically correct when we read: "And [Elohim] said, Let us make man in our image, after our likeness" (Genesis 1:26).

The Book of Genesis does not attempt to prove the existence of God. It forcefully presents the only eternal God as the Cause and the Creator of the universe in which we live. In the very first verse of the Bible we are given God's primary name, and from it, a glimpse of His power and majesty.

Next we need to consider exactly what God did when He created the heaven and the earth. *Created* is the English translation of the Hebrew *bara*. It means to bring into existence without the use of preexisting material, or from nothingness! This is true creation, and it cannot be studied or explained. It is an act beyond human achievement. In its fullest sense, we must recognize that finite human beings cannot create. We can study matter. We can even break it down into its component parts. We can change its shape. We can dissect, combine, gasify, and dissolve it. But we cannot create or destroy a single element that God made in the beginning.

The word *bara* quickly puts to rest, once and for all, the entire theory of evolution. Matter cannot evolve from nothing! In the beginning there had to be a Creator.

Bara is not used again until the fifth day of God's work: "And God created great whales, and every living creature that moveth, which the waters brought forth abundantly, after their kind, and every winged fowl after his kind" (Genesis 1:21).

This creative work continued into the sixth day, where the appearance of land animals is described. The Scriptures again refute one of the theories of evolution, that all life originated in the sea. Note carefully the Scriptural exegesis: "And God said, Let the *earth* bring forth the living creature after his kind, cattle, and creeping thing, and beast of the earth after his kind" (Genesis 1:24, italics added).

God's most important work, the creation of man, also occurred on the sixth day. This was to be a form of life made of the dust of the earth, but unique from all the others. Man was to be made or fashioned in God's own image and likeness: "And God said, Let us make man in our own image, after our likeness: and let them have dominion over the fish of the sea, and over the fowl of the air, and over the cattle, and over all the earth" (Genesis 1:26).

This superior life required a new act of creation, so the word *bara* is used again. "So God . . . created he him; male and female created he them" (Genesis 1:27).

Man did not evolve from either sea or land creatures. His appearance was an additional very special act of creation. His body was formed of the dust of the earth, but his spirit was from God.

"And the Lord God formed man of the dust of the ground, and breathed into his nostrils the breath of life; and man became a living soul" (Genesis 2:7).

The word *breath* is from the Hebrew *neshamah,* for spirit. Man, therefore, though temporarily clothed in an earthly body, is—like God—a spiritual being with an eternal destiny. God will someday create a new and heavenly body for each of His born again children. "And as we have borne the image of the earthy, we shall also bear the image of the heavenly" (1 Corinthians 15:49).

So the beginning referred to in the first verse of the first chapter of God's Holy Word is, in my point of view, the beginning of a chapter in the eternal reign of God, during which time He created a very special galaxy, a unique planet, and a creature called man, for whom He has eternal plans!

60

The Spirit of Man

But there is a spirit in man: and the inspiration of the Almighty giveth them understanding.

Job 32:8

God, the Holy Trinity (Father, Son, and Holy Spirit), made man in the image and likeness of Himself. We are, therefore, triune beings composed of a body, a soul, and a spirit. The "inspiration of the Almighty" means the breath of God; God breathed into the nostrils of Adam and he "became a living soul" (Genesis 2:7). The spirit is God-breathed. Significantly, it is recorded in the New Testament that God breathed on the apostles when He gave them His own Holy Spirit. "And when he had said this, he breathed on them, and saith unto them, Receive ye the Holy Ghost" (John 20:22).

It is not recorded in Scripture that God breathed on the animals, the fowls of the air, or the fish of the sea. Only man was so uniquely endowed that he might understand his special relationship to God and have spiritual fellowship with God! "God is a Spirit: and they that worship him must worship him in spirit and in truth" (John 4:24).

Adam enjoyed that special relationship for a while. He walked and talked with God in the garden. But God had warned Adam not to eat of the tree of the knowledge of good and evil, "for in the day that thou eatest thereof thou shalt surely die" (Genesis 2:17). Now Adam's body didn't die the day he disobeyed God, but his spiritual fellowship did. He could no longer walk and talk with God, and he was barred from any further access to the tree of life. He was spiritually dead because of his disobedience, and he began to die physically.

Adam's family, including us, were not born in the image and likeness of God; we were born in the image and likeness of Adam. "And Adam lived an hundred and thirty years, and begat a son in his own likeness, after his image; and called his name Seth" (Genesis 5:3).

That is why we all must be born again! We must be reborn spiritually to gain what Adam and Eve lost. "That which is born of the flesh is flesh; and that which is born of the Spirit is spirit" (John 3:6).

Until we are born again into the family of God, our spirits are dead in trespasses and sin, but the Holy Spirit of God "quickens" us, gives us new life. Our spirits are revived and our fellowship with God is restored. More than this, the Holy Spirit of God actually takes up residence within us, and we can never die spiritually again! "The Spirit itself beareth witness with our spirit, that we are the children of God" (Romans 8:16).

Many have asked, "What is the difference between the soul and the spirit of a man?" I believe that the soul is the awareness of life. Plant life, for example, is unconscious life. Plants have bodies, they are alive, they reproduce, and they die; but plants have no awareness of life or feeling. The next higher forms of life God created were the birds, the fish, and the animals. They are living creatures who are very much aware of their existence. They have feelings. They have souls. "But ask now the beasts, and they shall teach thee; and the fowls of the air, and they shall tell thee ... Who knoweth not in all these that the hand of the Lord hath wrought this? In whose hand is the soul of every living thing, and the breath of all mankind" (Job 12:7, 9, 10).

When an animal dies, the soul—or its awareness of life—dies with it. But man is a much higher form of life. Originally made in the likeness of God, he has a soul *and* a spirit. The spirit of man is what makes him Godlike. It is the spirit in man that sets him apart from all other forms of life. It is the spirit of man that finds joy and fulfillment in a right relationship with God! Man seeks to worship God; the animals have no such desire. It is the spirit of man that keeps the soul alive even after the body is dead. It is the spirit of man that, like his Creator, was made to live forever. For as I understand the Scriptures, the spirit can never really die. Though it may be dead in trespasses and sins, separated from fellowship with God, it still must return to God someday and give account! "Then shall the dust return to the earth as it was: and the spirit shall return unto God who gave it" (Ecclesiastes 12:7).

So often when someone dies we hear people say, "Now he is at peace . . . no more pain . . . at last his troubles are all behind him." The terrible tragedy of it all is the fact that these truths apply only to born again children of God! The vast majority of the dead are not at peace; they are in torment. This is because the death of the body is not the cessation of the awareness of life. Because we are like God, we can never really die. Our souls are just as aware of life when our bodies return to the dust of the earth as they ever were, because we have an eternal spirit. And if we are not saved, our souls are in hell, awaiting the judgment of God! "And in hell he lift up his eyes, being in torments" (Luke 16:23).

"The wicked shall be turned into hell, and all the nations that forget God" (Psalms 9:17).

But if we have been born again, when we die, our spirits ascend to the Lord, and our souls are indeed at peace. "We are confident, I say, and willing rather to be absent from the body, and to be present with the Lord" (2 Corinthians 5:8).

"Into thine hand I commit my spirit: thou hast redeemed me, O Lord God of truth" (Psalms 31:5).

The Scriptures make it very clear that the souls in hell and the souls in heaven are both looking forward to the resurrection of their bodies. The unsaved are looking forward to the occasion with dread and fear at the judgment of God. The saved are looking forward to the event with joyous anticipation.

"Marvel not at this: for the hour is coming, in the which all that are in the graves shall hear his voice. And shall come forth; they that have done good, unto the resurrection of life; and they that have done evil, unto the resurrection of damnation" (John 5:28, 29).

Of the unsaved, God has said: "And I saw the dead, small and great, stand before God; and the books were opened . . . And whosoever was not found written in the book of life was cast into the lake of fire "(Revelation 20:12, 15).

"And the devil that deceived them was cast into the lake of fire and brimstone, where the beast and the false prophet are, and shall be tormented day and night for ever and ever" (Revelation 20:10).

But God has promised the born-again that their bodies shall be resurrected to meet Him in the air and their spirits and souls will be joined together in new and glorified bodies, like unto the body of Christ. Of course there are those who may still be alive at the coming of the Lord. The Bible tells us their bodies will be transformed into

His likeness as they rise to meet Him. "Then we which are alive and remain shall be caught up together with them in the clouds" (1 Thessalonians 4:17).

"Beloved, now are we the sons of God, and it doth not yet appear what we shall be: but we know that, when he shall appear, we shall be like him; for we shall see him as he is" (1 John 3:2).

Until then, we should know that even in our imperfect state we are spiritual beings, originally created in the image and likeness of God, and though the image has been marred by sin, we have eternal destinies.

God has done all that He can do to redeem us. He wants us to live with Him forever. We can if we will accept His unspeakable gift. "And the very God of peace sanctify you wholly; and I pray God your whole spirit and soul and body be preserved blameless unto the coming of our Lord Jesus Christ" (1 Thessalonians 5:23).

61

Intercessory Prayer

The effectual fervent prayer of a righteous man availeth much.

James 5:16

I have never considered myself a great prayer warrior. In fact I often feel that I am missing something in my Christian experience when I hear how others have "prayed it through." I admire those who have prayed all night to find answers to their particular dilemmas. I confess that I have never even tried to pray that long. When praying, I'm just not much of a talker.

I know that our Lord prayed all night on occasion, but He knew what He was talking about! He is omniscient. He was discussing eternal matters with His heavenly Father that are humanly inexplicable. He was commiserating with and praying about the weaknesses of all His chosen ones from the beginning of time. Instead of growing weary, He was strengthened and refreshed by the time He spent in prayer. No wonder one of His disciples said, "Lord, teach us to pray." He then gave them some very explicit instructions about prayer and a significantly short model prayer.

I have a problem with those who say God answered their prayer when on occasion they received exactly what they asked for; conversely, they assume God didn't answer when they don't receive what they explicitly requested. Isn't it more likely that it was not our Father's will to grant their request? Does a good parent give a child everything he asks for? I think God answers all the prayers of His children in accordance with His will, His plan for our lives, and our own particular need. I'm so glad He does!

I know too that we often pray amiss. We ask God to do the very works that He has given us to do. We need to pray more often, "Here am I, Lord. Send me or use me." We need to pray for wisdom to recognize our own spiritual gifts and the works that He has already empowered us to do. We need to do our part in the miracles we seek.

There are times when we should recognize that God cannot grant the miracle we ask. Jesus was handicapped in His hometown of Nazareth because of their unbelief. "And he could there do no mighty work, save that he laid his hands upon a few sick folk, and healed them" (Mark 6:5).

We cannot, for example, pray a lost soul into the family of God if he will not believe. We can only pray for the convicting power of the Holy Spirit to come upon him, for wisdom to make our witness effective, for patience, and for God's love to be seen in us.

However, despite our frailties, we are commanded to "pray one for another, that ye may be healed" (James 5:16). Regardless of our limitations, we are called to be intercessors for the lost and for brethren in distress. What then are the secrets of successful intercessory prayer?

One thing I have learned is that real prayer is communication. I doubt that Jesus talked all night when He prayed. I'm sure He listened to His heavenly Father. So should we. In His instructions regarding prayer, Jesus advised us not to use "vain repetitions, as the heathen do: for they think that they shall be heard for their much speaking" (Matthew 6:7).

My most enjoyable and rewarding prayers are a combination of talking to God and meditating. I believe we should read a portion of His Word during our prayer time. We should ask the Holy Spirit for wisdom and meditate on the Scripture we have read. That's how God talks to us!

I also know that intercessory prayer requires a right relationship with God the Holy Spirit. We need to be filled with the Spirit. This requires self-examination, confession of sin in our lives, repentance, and awareness of God's forgiveness.

How can we intercede for others if we fail to acknowledge our own frailties? If we have quenched the Holy Spirit in our daily activities, we cannot know His will or pray in Jesus' name until that right relationship is completely restored! If we have been too busy to pray without ceasing, and if the awareness of God's presence has not filled our hearts and our thoughts throughout the day, then we are not prepared to pray for others. Church attendance is not enough. We can be involved in all kinds of religious activity and yet be without empathy with our Father's will. To be an intercessor, our hearts must be right with God and our senses tuned to the direction of His Holy Spirit.

"Wherefore the Lord said, Forasmuch as this people draw near me with their mouth, and with their lips do honour me, but have removed their heart far from me, and their fear toward me is taught by the precept of men." (Isaiah 29:13).

Sometimes our prayers are so routine that we can scarcely stay awake while praying, and I think even our sympathetic heavenly Father must have to suppress a yawn. Certainly we would lose the attention of our family if we held such conversations with them. Intercessors must be genuinely and spiritually concerned. Again this involves the condition of our hearts. I don't think the words we speak are nearly as important as the concern God sees in our hearts!

Intercessory prayer therefore demands sincerity. We don't pray for someone just because we were asked to; we pray because we sincerely care. When we are asked to pray for others, we need to know something about them. Do they know our Lord? Do they believe and trust in Him? What have they done concerning the problem? Is there anything we can and should do besides praying? We, as members of the body of Christ, are already empowered by the Spirit of God to do many good works. We should have the faith to do them.

I am reminded of the scriptural account of some men who brought to Jesus a friend who was sick with the palsy. They could not enter the house where Jesus was because of the multitude, so they climbed up on the roof, removed the roof tiling, and lowered their friend down to the feet of the Lord. First they did all they could do, then they believed that Jesus would do the rest! "And when he [Jesus] saw their faith, he said unto him [the sick of the palsy] Man, thy sins are forgiven thee" (Luke 5:20).

These men sincerely loved their friend, and their actions epitomize intercessory prayer in action. Genuine love begets sincerity. We recognize too that our own personal love for others is insufficient. We must have God's agape love in our hearts if we desire to do the work of an intercessor! The shortest and the most overlooked verse in the Bible is, "Jesus wept" (John 11:35). I confess to God that I have not wept much in my prayers for others. Have you?

The final necessary ingredient in successful intercessory prayer is faith. The foregoing Scripture tells us that when Jesus saw their faith, He proceeded to heal their friend. So many of those in the modern healing ministry tend to glorify themselves when a patient is apparently healed, but when they fail, they point to their patient's lack of faith. It's an easy out. Our Lord Jesus is our model intercessor, and His success is certainly not dependent on man's great faith! He forgives our lack of faith. He is the greatest and most faithful of all intercessors. If we would be intercessors, we must emulate Him. This is what He meant when He instructed us to pray in His name. It is not just a matter of faithfully saying the words *in Jesus' name* at the close of our prayer, but recognizing that we are praying as His personal representatives. We are to have the mind of Christ, so our prayer is actually His prayer. This is the kind of faith we must contend for.

How can we develop the faith necessary to really pray in Jesus' name? I think it comes with practice. When we were saved, it was through a simple childlike faith given to us by God. "For by grace are ye saved through faith; and that not of yourselves: it is the gift of God" (Ephesians 2:8).

That tiny seed of faith grows as we grow spiritually, as we feed on the Word of God and become obedient "doers of the word, and not hearers only" (James 1:22). Jesus said, "Why call ye me, Lord, Lord, and do not the things which I say?" (Luke 6:46). Our faith grows as we prove by our experiences as doers that God keeps His promises! Faith cannot develop in an inactive Christian. Faith is the result of obedient service, and it compounds as we experience the results.

It is my point of view that successful intercessory prayer requires these hard-sought ingredients:

- Communication with God
- A right relationship with the Holy Spirit
- Sincerity
- God's love in our hearts
- Personal faith

It won't come easy. It will cost us time and tears to acquire these attributes, but it will be worth it all. I believe it to be the crowning achievement of the Christian pilgrimage.

Finally, I will not sidestep the much maligned spiritual gift of healing. The apostles of our Lord administered it with great power simply by the laying on of hands. I believe that kind of power passed away with the death of the apostles. However, all of God's children are called to be disciples, to do the work of the Lord's church, to be intercessors, and this includes prayers for the sick.

> Is any sick among you? let him call for the elders of the church; and let them pray over him, anointing him with oil in the name of the Lord: And the prayer of faith shall save the sick, and the Lord shall raise him up; and if he have committed sins, they shall be forgiven him. Confess your faults one to another, and pray one for another, that ye may be healed. The effectual fervent prayer of a righteous man availeth much.
>
> James 5:14-16

All of God's children are called to be intercessors. We, and especially the elders in the church, ought to be much more involved in the ministries of prayer and healing in these last days.

62
World Peace

The leaders of the nations met
And so decided to create
A worldwide league of great intrigue
To banish every warlike state.

"We shall police the world," they planned,
"That no insurgent party rise
To conflagrate the earth with hate,
That in our might our safety lies."

But then with might, what fools have tried
To subjugate the world and died,
For might of man since time began
Has never stemmed the evil tide.

Oh, would to God that we might see,
On bended knees, in humble prayer,
The high command of every land
With arms around each other there.

Beseeching guidance in a plan
That peace on earth might so remain,
That mankind's grief might find relief,
That men shall not have died in vain.

63

The Act of Worship

O come, let us worship and bow down: let us kneel before the Lord our maker.

Psalms 95:6

All human beings instinctively and intuitively know that there is a God and that we must have a right relationship with Him. The human soul is lonely and cannot find fulfillment until that right relationship is achieved. The ultimate human experience upon knowing God is to worship Him. This is the birthright of all God's children.

When we are truly born again into the family of God, we begin that new and right relationship with exhilaration and a genuine enthusiasm. We desire to feed on the Word, that we may grow thereby, and to bring glory to God by the way we live. However, the exhilaration soon falls flat and the enthusiasm dwindles as the salvation experience fades swiftly into the past. We soon fall into the humdrum experience of only "going to church."

Too often we exacerbate the dullness by criticizing the pastor, his sermons, the choir, and even other members of the congregation. Somehow in our quest for spiritual enrichment and a continuance of the joy of our salvation, we have left our first love (*see* Revelation 2:4). Who and what are to blame?

I believe that a Christian cannot "go to church." We need to remember that *we are the church* wherever we go. We have work to do. There will be problems and disappointments and tears. Our Lord never said that following Him would always be joyful and exciting. Certainly, we should not expect the local church to provide weekly entertainment! Then why do we assemble ourselves? Isn't the first and foremost reason to worship God? Yes, but we seldom do!

We use the local church building for many useful purposes: to study the Word, to hear it preached, to utilize the talents of our members and the gifts of the Holy Spirit, to bring our unsaved friends under the sound of the Gospel, to bring our tithes and offerings to the Lord, to establish and support the work of missionaries, and for Christian fellowship. But when and how do we worship in spirit and truth? We are all too often denied that enriching experience which is the Christian's birthright.

What is worship? Is it not the directing of our thoughts and the love in our hearts toward God? Isn't it offering our sacrifices of praise as a sweet-smelling savor? Isn't it giving thanks to the Lamb of God for the blood that bought us? Worship is something *we do.* Most church services deny us this privilege, and we come away feeling empty and deprived.

Generally we are preached at. We have become more of an audience than a congregation. Much of the sermon content is directed to the unsaved and/or backsliders. Many messages directed to the flock admonish us for our shortcomings. The remainder are sermons intended to uplift and exhilarate us. These are now the most popular, for we all have "itching ears" (*see* 2 Timothy 4:3). We want to come away from the service feeling good about ourselves, and we enjoy being entertained. The pastor is expected to be witty and have a good sense of humor. The special music is for our enjoyment. It is announced that, "Mrs. Jones will now play or sing for us." Small wonder that in many churches the audiences now applaud the entertainers! Pastors generally use the closing prayer for a final appeal for a reaction of some sort from their audience.

I submit that a worship service should be more. True public worship is something the congregation does. We offer up our prayers to the Lord. We sing for His glory and for His pleasure. The sermon should praise Him and offer up our thanksgiving. The entire service should have the objective of praise, joy, and love toward God. In a true worship service, we are not the audience, God is! When God the Father, God the Son, and God the Holy Spirit are glorified in worship by an assembly of believers, even the angels of heaven join in. That's the way the early church worshiped. It was almost like being in heaven!

> And I beheld, and I heard the voice of many angels round about the throne and the beasts and the elders: and the number of them was ten thousand times ten thousand, and thousands of thousands; Saying with a loud voice, Worthy

is the Lamb that was slain to receive power, and riches, and wisdom, and strength, and honour, and glory, and blessing. And every creature which is in heaven, and on the earth, and under the earth, and such as are in the sea, and all that are in them, heard I saying, Blessing, and honour, and glory, and power, be unto him that sitteth upon the throne, and unto the Lamb for ever and ever.

Revelation 5:11-13

Worshiping God in spirit and in truth is not only a sweet-smelling savor unto Him, but it thrills our own hearts so that we overflow with the joy of heaven. True worship begets radiant Christians, and that's what the world needs to see.

I acknowledge the need for preaching, "For the preaching of the cross is to them that perish foolishness; but unto us which are saved it is the power of God" (1 Corinthians 1:18). But it must allow and provide the spirit of worship. A good sermon should include the ingredients of praise, thanksgiving, exhortation, warning, and the sweet, simple message of the Gospel. Christians need to feed on the Word of God, and the world needs to hear it. But again, the Sunday services in many churches seem to have lost the reverent and worshipful atmosphere we so urgently need.

Some churches have helped by making the Sunday morning service more of a worship service while reserving the evening service for evangelical outreach. Many, however, have dropped the evening service altogether. The pastor's opportunities to meet the needs of his congregation are therefore limited. Some pastors have become preachers only in the desperation to revive the flock. Consequently, we are missing the blessings of worship. We are spiritually deprived. We are not enjoying our birthright. That's why going to church gets dull.

Before the early apostolic churches left their first love, the Word of the Lord was preached in the streets and marketplaces of the world, and when the saints assembled themselves, it was to praise God in the ecstasy of worship. The Scriptures record that on occasion, "the place was shaken where they were assembled together; and they were all filled with the Holy Ghost" (Acts 4:31). We need to revive the act of worship.

64

Christians With Dirty Feet

Jesus saith to him, He that is washed needeth not save to wash his feet.

John 13:10

Recently our Bible class teacher asked what the Lord meant when He said, "Except a man be born of water and of the Spirit, he cannot enter into the kingdom of God" (John 3:5). Many in the class felt this was a reference to water baptism. If this were true, then baptism would be a requisite of the salvation experience. Others in the class felt that the mention of water was an allusion to our natural birth, which is subsequently succeeded by our spiritual rebirth. Neither of these explanations seemed credible or germane to the issue. I believe that Jesus was describing two intrinsic and distinct requirements of the new birth.

Water in the Bible is a symbol of refreshing, cleansing, and renewal. It is essential to life. Water provides nourishment and renewal to the land; it is the Lord's metaphor for the spiritual cleansing of a nation. The "washing of water by the Word" awakens, convicts, and cleanses the repentant human soul! The prophet Ezekiel, speaking for God, prophesied to the nation of Israel:

For I will take you from among the heathen, and gather you out of all countries, and will bring you into your land. Then will I sprinkle clean water upon you, and ye shall be clean: from all your filthiness, and from all your idols, will I cleanse you. A new heart also will I give you, and a new spirit will I put within you: and I will take away the stony heart out of your flesh, and I will give you an heart of flesh. And I will put my spirit within you, and cause you to walk in my statutes, and ye shall keep my judgments, and do them.

Ezekiel 36:24-27

This is a reference to the future rebirth of the nation of Israel. Please note that they will be born again of both *water and the Spirit!* The same is true of every born again believer.

Jesus also said to His disciples, "Now ye are clean through the word which I have spoken unto you" (John 15:3). This amply illustrates that it is by God's Word we sense the need for confession and repentance, and consequently come to Christ and are cleansed. If we had never heard or read the Holy Word, we could not have been reborn. The Apostle Paul wrote that the church is sanctified and cleansed by the "washing of water by the word" (Ephesians 5:26). The cleansing power of the Word of God (the water) and the power of the Holy Spirit are both prerequisites of the new birth. Paul reinforced this truth in the Epistle to Titus, where he wrote, "Not by works of righteousness which we have done, but according to his mercy he saved us, by the washing of regeneration, and renewing of the Holy Ghost" (Titus 3:5).

When Jesus washed the disciples' feet, He meant it to be more than a lesson in humility. It was to exemplify an importunate need in their Christian life and service. The Oriental custom of foot washing was observed by every good host in Jesus' time. Due to the fact that open-toed sandals were worn and the roads were dusty, the feet of all travelers needed washing. Even after a visit to the public baths, their feet needed washing again.

The lesson applies to all who would follow our Lord. Our salvation is secure because He has "washed us from our sins in his own blood" (Revelation 1:5). Positionally, we are cleansed from all our sins: past, present, and future. However, in our daily walk we get our feet dirty. We become defiled by the sins that so easily beset us. We fail our Lord in a hundred different ways. Our light doesn't shine for His glory. We are not the salt of the earth that we ought to be. We all continue to come short of the glory of God. We need to deal with the sin in our lives now, or our Lord will have to deal with it at the judgment seat. We who are truly born again will not lose our salvation because of our sins, but we will have to give account, and we will lose rewards. We are Christians with dirty feet!

So what must we do? We need to wash our feet daily. We do so by confessing our sins to the Lord and by repenting so that our fellowship with the Father, the Son, and the Holy Spirit is not interrupted. If we ignore our sins, we grieve His Holy Spirit and cannot effectively serve God. Our Lord's finished work has sanctified us for heaven, but we must sanctify ourselves for service! Significantly, Joshua commanded the people of Israel before they entered the Holy Land, "Sanctify yourselves: for to morrow the Lord will do wonders among you" (Joshua 3:5).

God cannot use unclean vessels!

Jesus also said, "If I then, your Lord and Master, have washed your feet; ye also ought to wash one another's feet" (John 13:14). Some churches take this literally and actually conduct foot washing services. I think our Lord had more than this in mind. I think He was exemplifying something more than humility. He wants our service to be humble, of course, but He also wants us to bear fruit. He wants us to be vessels fit for the Master's use. Perhaps the Apostle James understood it best, for he wrote: "Confess your faults one to another, and pray one for another, that ye may be healed" (James 5:16).

I think this is washing one another's feet in the truest sense!

Finally, the Apostle John confirms the great truth that the Spirit, the water, and the blood are a holy trinity, the substantive elements of God's perfect work. All are involved in the salvation of the human soul.

"For there are three that bear record in heaven, The Father, the Word, and the Holy Ghost: and these three are one. And there are three that bear witness in earth, the spirit, and the water, and the blood: and these three agree in one" (1 John 5:7, 8).

This, I believe, is a Scriptural exegesis of all that our Lord meant to convey when He said, "Except a man be born of water and of the Spirit, he cannot enter into the kingdom of God" (John 3:5). Thank God we don't have to understand it all now, but someday we will. Someday our knowledge of the written Word will no longer be clouded by the limitations of our finite minds. We shall then know the Living Word, even as we are known now. We shall be like Him, and our feet will never get dirty again.

65

Resurrection Sunday

Easter

And there are also many other things which Jesus did, the which, if they should be written every one, I suppose that even the world itself could not contain the books that should be written. Amen.

John 21:25

The greatest single event in the history of planet earth was the resurrection of our Lord Jesus Christ from the dead. If it had not occurred, His birth, His momentous life, the miracles He performed, and His death would have soon been forgotten, This greatest of events is also the most remembered, most documented, and most authenticated event in all of recorded history. What more could God do to prove the truth of life after death than this?

All the Old Testament prophecies concerning the first coming of Messiah have been fulfilled in every detail. No honest research of the Holy Scriptures could lead to any other conclusion than that Jesus Christ was God in human flesh, and that "he is risen, as he said" (Matthew 28:6). The Gospel writers all told their own versions of His life, death, and resurrection. All agree, though some recount more of the details, and all excitedly confirm our Lord's fulfillment of the ancient prophecies. The Apostle John concluded his Gospel by say it is just not possible to relate all the wonderful things that should be said regarding the short life of our Savior.

But again, the most important event was our Lord's resurrection. All of the precautions of man and the power of Rome could not prevent it. Christianity is the only religion whose founder was dead, is alive, and is coming again! May I share with you just a few of the Scriptures confirming prophecies fulfilled and the undeniable proofs that we serve a risen Lord?

173

First there is a type of the bodily resurrection of Jesus given to Israel in the Feast of the Firstfruits:

And the Lord spake unto Moses, saying, Speak unto the children of Israel, and say unto them, When ye be come into the land which I give unto you, and shall reap the harvest thereof, then ye shall bring a sheaf of the firstfruits of your harvest unto the priest: And he shall wave the sheaf before the Lord, to be accepted for you: on the morrow after the sabbath the priest shall wave it.

Leviticus 23:9-11

The firstfruits were a prelude of the harvest yet to come, and please note that a sheaf of the firstfruits was to be waved before the Lord on the morning after the Sabbath. Our Lord was resurrected in exact fulfillment of that type on Sunday, which we forever after call the Lord's Day! He is the "firstfruits of them that sleep" (*see* 1 Corinthians 15:20-23) and of the great harvest which shall follow!

Now the Old Testament sheaf was plural. Though a single seed was sown, it would bring forth multiple blossoms and fruit. And so again the type was exactly fulfilled. There were multiple bodily resurrections on that first Lord's Day.

And, behold, the veil of the temple was rent in twain from the top to the bottom; and the earth did quake, and the rocks rent; And the graves were opened; and many bodies of the saints which slept arose, And came out of the graves after his resurrection, and went into the holy city, and appeared unto many.

Matthew 27:51-53

Note that although the Lord's death on Friday opened the graves, there were no resurrections until the Lord's Day. They had to wait for their High Priest to present them (the wave sheaf) before the Father in heaven—again, in exact fulfillment of the Old Testament type. I believe the Lord ascended bodily on the third day to present a sheaf of the Old Testament saints to the Father. Remember His words to Mary Magdalene, who saw Him first after His resurrection? "Jesus saith unto her, Touch me not [don't hinder Me now]; for I am not yet ascended to my Father: but go to my brethren, and say unto them, I ascend unto my Father, and your Father; and to my God, and your God" (John 20:17).

I believe that our Lord also freed all the *spirits* of the Old Testament saints who were waiting in paradise (Abraham's bosom, *see* Luke 16:22), looking for His coming. These saved living spirits could not go to heaven until the price for sin had first been paid, but they were comforted in the knowledge that their Messiah would come. Remember the words of our Lord just before His death as He turned to the believing thief on the cross next to Him: "Verily I say unto thee, Today shalt thou be with me in paradise" (Luke 23:43). We can believe from this that when Christ dismissed His Spirit, He went to paradise that very day and took the spirit of the believing thief with Him. What a day of rejoicing that must have been for the saints in paradise. The Apostle Paul wrote of their freedom from the captivity of death in his Epistle to the Ephesians, "When he [Jesus] ascended up on high, he led captivity captive" (Ephesians 4:8).

Then, on the third day, our Lord and certain of the Old Testament saints were raised *bodily*.

Jesus, our great High Priest, waved this sheaf of firstfruits before the Father and returned to earth to assure the apostles and all His followers that He had, indeed, risen as He said. From the accounts in each of the Gospels, the order of His appearances was as follows:

It was Mary Magdalene who first saw the Lord (Mark 16:9). Then the other women who had brought the spices and ointments and found the tomb empty (Matthew 28:9). The first of the apostles to see Him was Peter (Luke 24:34). This is confirmed in 1 Corinthians 15:5. Peter had denied his Lord and perhaps Jesus, aware of Peter's remorse, sought him out for this reason. After Peter, He was seen by two of His disciples on the road to Emmaus (Luke 24:13-32), and then by all of the apostles (with the exception of Thomas) in the upper room (John 20:19-23).

Eight days later He was seen again by the apostles including Thomas (John 20:26-29). It was at this appearance that doubting Thomas confirmed that Jesus was both Lord and God! No mortal man could so materialize through locked doors and impervious walls! Later, in Galilee, He appeared to seven of the apostles by the sea of Tiberias (John 21:1-12).

Next, He appeared to the apostles and five hundred of the brethren (1 Corinthians 15:6), then to James alone. James seems to have been the leader of the church at Jerusalem (Acts 15:13-21). And finally, our Lord was last seen by the apostles when He ascended into heaven from the Mount of Olives (Acts 1:1-11). This was undoubtedly the most glorious and reassuring experience of all for the apostles, and they returned to Jerusalem without fear and with great faith to await their empowerment by the Holy Spirit.

Christ remained on earth forty days after His resurrection, showing Himself alive by many infallible proofs. He opened the Old Testament Scriptures to His disciples, showing Himself as the fulfillment of God's promises to the patriarchs. I think it is significant that He only appeared to believers. These were not extraordinarily brave men and women who wanted to die as martyrs! They were, at first, frightened and lacking in faith, but when they saw and touched with their own hands the risen Savior, they were never afraid again. And with unparalleled faith they went out and "turned the world upside down" (Acts 17:6) for Jesus Christ. When Christ comes again to call out His holy church, He will appear only to those who are looking for His coming (*see* Hebrews 9:28). The unsaved will not see Christ until He returns to judge them.

Finally, there was one man who never understood it all or never had the opportunity to hear and comprehend all the infallible proofs regarding Jesus as the promised Messiah of Israel. But he was the one in charge when Jesus was crucified. He had witnessed His unique death; he experienced the blackness that engulfed the earth; he trembled as the earth quaked beneath his feet; he witnessed the graves opening and all "these things that were done." He was a Roman centurion, and he and his men feared greatly and pronounced to our unbelieving world, "Truly this was the Son of God!" (Matthew 27:54).

66

When Was Our Lord in The Heart of the Earth?

For as Jonas was three days and three nights in the whale's belly; so shall the Son of man be three days and three nights in the heart of the earth.

Matthew 12:40

Many pastors and teachers have confused their constituents by interpreting the "heart of the earth" as the grave. Consequently, they are forced to the conclusion that Jesus was buried on Thursday instead of Friday in order to fulfill His own prophecy of spending three nights in the earth. However, the scriptural accounts of His burial and resurrection make it abundantly clear that He died on the traditional Good Friday, as the church has always believed, and that His body was indeed only two nights in the grave. Let's look at the account from the Gospel of Luke.

And that day [Friday] was the preparation, and the sabbath drew on. And the women also, which came with him from Galilee, followed after, and beheld the sepulchre, and how his body was laid. And they returned, and prepared spices and ointments; and rested the sabbath day [Saturday] according to the commandment.

Luke 23:54-56

Now upon the first day of the week [Sunday], very early in the morning, they came unto the sepulchre.

Luke 24:1

Notice that the women rested only a single "day," not two days, as I have heard some explain.

I believe Jesus descended to "the heart of the earth" during His prayers to the Father in the Garden of Gethsemane. When He said, "Not my will but thine be done," He was made earthy, like Adam and all sinful humanity. Like Adam, He was separated from the Father [He died spiritually] when God "laid on him the iniquity of us all" (Isaiah 53:6).

"For he hath made him to be sin for us, who knew no sin; that we might be made the righteousness of God in him" (2 Corinthians 5:21).

"And as we [and He] have borne the image of the earthy [the first Adam], we shall also bear the image of the heavenly [Jesus, the last Adam]" (1 Corinthians 15:49).

So the earthy travail of our Savior's soul began that Thursday evening as He, bearing our sins in His previously sinless body, turned Himself over to His captors.

Before we expound further regarding this interpretation, let's look at some corroborating Old Testament Scriptures.

"Thou, which hast shewed me great and sore troubles shalt quicken me again, and shalt bring me up again from the depths of the earth" (Psalms 71:20).

Taken out of its context, we might assume that "depths of the earth" is a reference to the grave. But David was not referring to his death. He was lamenting the afflictions he had endured at the hands of wicked adversaries. Note verse 4 of the same chapter: "Deliver me, O my God, out of the hand of the wicked, out of the hand of the unrighteous and cruel man" (Psalms 71:4).

Also note the following allusion to the psalmist's earthy estate: "My substance was not hid from thee, when I was made in secret, and curiously wrought in the lowest parts of the earth" (Psalms 139:15).

This is a reference to his creation, not his death. I think he used the term "lowest parts of the earth" in humble recognition of his Adamic nature.

Jonah's experience in the belly of the great fish was not of death and the grave, even though he feared they would be the ultimate consequences. For three days and three nights he endured the judgment of God. Like our Savior, he turned himself over to his captors and was cast into the depths. He felt that God had forsaken him and that he was alone in the heart of the earth. "Then I said, I am cast out of thy sight . . . I went down to the bottoms of the mountains; the earth with her bars was about me for ever: yet hast thou brought up my life from corruption, O Lord my God" (Jonah 2:4, 6).

The Apostle Paul used similar phraseology regarding our Lord's travail: "Now that he ascended, what is it but that he also descended first into the lower parts of the earth?" (Ephesians 4:9).

The Lord's suffering for our sins did not begin on the cross. It began on that fateful night in the Garden of Gethsemane when He sweat great drops of blood. (Remember, it is by the shedding of His precious blood that we are redeemed, and not by His death alone.) His cross included *all* that He endured to secure our redemption, even as the cross we bear is all that we suffer for Him.

He suffered alone. We cannot share in the bearing of His cross. Jesus paid it all. His disciples fled when He allowed Himself to be taken captive. Alone, He was despitefully used. His tormentors blindfolded Him, spit on Him, and tore out pieces of His beard. They beat Him and mocked Him as He was paraded before the high priest. Like Jonah, He went down "to the bottoms of the mountains."

The next day, Friday, He was jeered and ridiculed as they led Him to Pilate, then to Herod, and back to Pilate again. He was scourged (beaten with thongs of leather, sometimes with pieces of metal fastened to them) nearly to death. He was stripped of His clothing, and they put on Him a scarlet robe. A crown of cruel thorns was pressed upon His head, and He was given a reed for a scepter, then they mocked Him, saying, "Hail, King of the Jews." They then spit on Him and smote Him with the reed (more like what we would call a rod). Finally they took Him outside the gates of the city and crucified Him.

The prophet Isaiah has written that our Lord was so bloody and battered that He no longer had the appearance of a son of man. "his visage was so marred more than any man, and his form more than the sons of men" (Isaiah 52:14).

And so our complete redemption was secured by all that He suffered, and not by His death on the cross alone.

> Surely he hath borne our griefs, and carried our sorrows: yet
> we did esteem him stricken, smitten of God, and afflicted.
> But he was wounded for our transgressions, he was bruised

for our iniquities: the chastisement of our peace was upon him; and with his stripes we are healed.

Isaiah 53:4, 5

Our Lord's physical suffering, however, is only part of all that He endured in the heart of the earth. More excruciatingly painful was the inexplicable sorrow of His complete separation from the Father. Like Jonah, He felt that He was abandoned by God the Father as He cried out from the cross, "My God, my God, why hast thou forsaken me?" (Matthew 27:46). His agony is vividly recorded in Psalms 22. Note particularly that the Son of Man was descended like a worm and relegated to the dust of the earth.

"But I am a worm, and no man; a reproach of men, and despised of the people" (Psalms 22:6).

"My strength is dried up like a potsherd; and my tongue cleaveth to my jaws; and thou hast brought me into the dust of death" (Psalms 22:15).

The Scriptures are also explicit that only our Lord's body entered the grave. He dismissed His Spirit while He was still on the cross, and His Spirit descended to a place where the Old Testament saints awaited His coming. Was hades in the lowest parts of the earth? Actually, this prison of departed spirits, both saved and unsaved, was in another dimension, intellectually fathomless and physically impenetrable. Certainly, it was not some physical location beneath the crust of this explorable earth, but a place where only departed spirits can enter. (The spirits of the unsaved are still there. Their portion of hades is hell.) It is a place where only the *Spirit* of our Lord could enter, and victoriously He set the *spirits* of the ransomed captives free!

Finally, we should remember that the Hebrews reckoned the period of a day from evening to evening. As we read in Genesis 1:5, "the evening and the morning were the first day." Thus each new day began at sundown. Our Lord's heart of the earth experience, instead of beginning on Thursday night, actually began on their Friday. The three days and three nights by Hebrew reckoning were from sundown Friday to sundown Monday. I believe our Lord ended His earthly travail when He delivered the promised firstfruits (His own resurrected body and the bodies of many Old Testament saints) to the Father in heaven sometime before sundown on Sunday. This was the completion of three days and three nights in fulfillment of the Jonah type.

67

Innocence and the Age of Accountability

Verily I say unto you, Except ye be converted, and become as little children, ye shall not enter into the kingdom of heaven.
Matthew 18:3

Adam and Eve, created in the image and likeness of God, were for a while wholly innocent. They did not even know there was such a thing as sin. As innocents they were able to fellowship with God as no other humans have. But it was not God's plan to keep them innocent. There was sin in the universe, and it had to be defeated. It was necessary for man to experience sin and to accept God's plan of victory over sin. His plan would make man perfect. His perfection is greater than innocence, and it will endure forever. "For by one offering he hath perfected for ever them that are sanctified" (Hebrews 10:14).

It is a popular Christian belief that all little children are innocent until they come to an age of accountability. This belief is nowhere substantiated in the Word of God. Since Adam and Eve brought down the human race, only Jesus was wholly innocent; all other children are born sinners. Consider the following declarations of the psalmist: "Behold, I was shaped in iniquity; and in sin did my mother conceive me" (Psalms 51:5).

I am reminded that when God sent the armies of Israel into the Promised Land, He commanded them to slay all the men, women, and even little children of all the nations that dwelt therein. "And the city shall be accursed, even it, and all that are therein" (Joshua 6:17).

"And they utterly destroyed all that was in the city, both man and woman, young and old" (Joshua 6:21).

"So Joshua smote all the country . . . and all their kings; he left none remaining, but utterly destroyed all that breathed, as the Lord God of Israel commanded" (Joshua 10:40).

Would God curse *innocent* children and then command that they be slain? I think not. The inhabitants of Canaan were unspeakably evil, and if they were allowed to cohabit with Israel, God's chosen people would be polluted. Israel's disobedience of this clear command contributed to their ultimate downfall.

So then, if all little children are sinners, what is the difference between the children of the heathen and the children of Christians? When infants die before they are old enough to believe and be born again, do they *all* go to hell? This was the concern of Old Testament saints, and it is rightly the concern of Christians today, and God *has provided a way of salvation for infants.*

Our Lord Jesus, in His discourse on little children, made reference to sheep in the fold: "If a man have an hundred sheep, and one of them be gone astray, doth he not leave the ninety and nine . . . and seeketh that which is gone astray? Even so it is not the will of your Father which is in heaven, that one of these little ones should perish" (Matthew 18:12, 14).

Old Testament saints sought to keep their children in the fold. They considered their children a blessing from God, praying for them before conception and afterward. They brought sacrifices to the temple to atone for their sinful natures. They dedicated themselves and their children to the Lord. They brought them up in the fear and admonition of the Lord, as Moses had commanded them. "And these words which I command thee this day shall be in thine heart, and thou shalt teach them diligently to thy children" (Deuteronomy 7:6, 7). And in Proverbs we read, "Train up a child in the way he should go: and when he is old, he will not depart from it" (Proverbs 22:6).

"Chasten thy son while there is hope and let not thy soul spare for his crying" (Proverbs 19:18).

In the church age we are similarly concerned, and so we too pray for our children before they are born. We dedicate ourselves to bringing them up as members of the family of God. We also try from the moment of conception to keep them as little sheep in the fold of God. We dedicated them and ourselves publicly at every opportunity to live for God and for His glory. Our intercessory prayers to God are to keep them from the Evil One. And as soon as they are able to understand, we teach them that Jesus, the Good Shepherd, is the Way, the Truth, and the Life.

The Apostle Paul further confirms the truth that we can be intercessors for our infant children. In fact, he states that even if only one of an infant's parents is a true believer, the child is holy (separated unto God). "For the unbelieving husband is sanctified by the [believing] wife, and the unbelieving wife is sanctified by the [believing] husband: else were your children unclean; but now are they holy" (1 Corinthians 7:14).

Some Christian denominations baptize their infants as a further precaution. However, all agree that the child must someday make his own confession of faith. Some state that their confirmation should be made at age twelve. However, the Bible does not teach that there is any saving power in baptism, nor is there any age given when a child actually becomes accountable. Jesus said, "Suffer little children to come unto me, and forbid them not" (Luke 18:16). I think this means, "Let them come to Me as quickly as they are able to comprehend the love of God!" I believe this applies to the very young. It is my point of view that the holy will of God is that we bring up our children so that they may never stray from the fold or need to be converted. We will teach them to believe in their hearts and confess with their mouths the Lord Jesus at the earliest age possible. When they do this, they are born again, and their position is secured.

Of course, there are always those children, even of Christian parents, who are never really in the fold. They will never truly love God, and they will break their parents' hearts. There are others who will, later in life, remember their childhood training and the prayers of their parents and turn again to the Lord. They were always in the fold, but only God could tell.

The age-old question regarding children in heathen lands is, "Why should they suffer in hell when they never had a chance to be saved?" Also, what of the adults who never heard the Gospel in all their lifetime? All of the unsaved are considered heathen in the Bible, including those in civilized lands who have heard but will not believe the love of God. Will they all suffer forever and ever in eternal hell? Are they all equally guilty?

The Bible clearly teaches that the unredeemed of the earth cannot inherit eternal life. They are already dead in sins and trespasses, and they are "without excuse" (Romans 1:20). They will be judged by the amount of light or understanding given them and by their works, and they will endure varying degrees of punishment: "And that servant, which knew his lord's will, and prepared not himself, neither did according to his will, shall be beaten with many stripes. But he that knew not, and did commit things worthy of stripes, shall be beaten with few stripes" (Luke 12:47, 48).

Let us be content to believe that God is just. He will do what is best and right. The Bible tells us that death and hell and all the unredeemed will be cast into the lake of fire that is God's final judgment. It is possible that the fire may mean only eternal death for some (such as heathen infants). We know that it will mean eternal suffering for Satan and his followers.

Finally, we should always remember that God is omniscient. He knew from the beginning of creation all those who are His. He knew those who would follow the way He would provide in every dispensation. And so He chose or predestinated them to someday conform to the image of His firstborn (*see* Romans 8:29). He wrote their names in the Lamb's book of life before the foundation of the world (*see* Ephesians 1:4, 5), and God has no eraser on His pencil!

God knows how every child who dies in infancy would have turned out if allowed to live longer. Let's leave the judgment to Him. Our concern as Christian parents should be to pray, teach, train, and so love our children that they may never know an unsaved moment!

68

Know Ye Not That Ye Are Gods?

Jesus answered them, Is it not written in your law, I said, Ye are gods?

John 10:34

We humans think of ourselves as mortals, and so we are. *Mortal* means we must eventually die. But there is a vast difference between what death means to mankind and what it means to all other living creatures.

We were all created originally from the dust of the earth, and as God has decreed, "unto dust shalt thou return" (Genesis 3:19). But mankind was also created in the image and likeness of God (Genesis 1:27), so we are more than dust.

When an animal dies, its soul (its awareness of life) also dies. Both body and soul are obliterated forever. But man has an eternal spirit that is the dwelling place of the human soul. Our bodies perish, but our awareness of life never ceases! When God created man, He "breathed into his nostrils the breath of life; and man became a living soul" (Genesis 2:7). The spirit is God-breathed. In the Gospel of John it is recorded that God breathed on certain of His followers again, that they might be partakers of His Holy Spirit. "And when he had said this, he breathed on them, and saith unto them, Receive ye the Holy Ghost" (John 20:22).

It is the spirit in man that makes him like God. We were meant for eternity. There is nothing in Holy Scripture to indicate that the spirit ever dies. That is why God called us gods. Both the spirits of the saved and the unsaved shall someday inhabit resurrected bodies prepared by God for judgment and an eternal existence. The saved will enjoy new and glorified bodies like that of our Lord's and will live with Him forever. The unsaved will face their Maker in bodies prepared for condemnation.

"Marvel not at this: for the hour is coming, in the which all that are in the graves shall hear his voice, And shall come forth; they that have done good, unto the resurrection of life; and they that have done evil, unto the resurrection of damnation" (John 5:28, 29).

The Bible tells us that when our bodies are consigned to the gave, our spirits and souls are as alive as they ever were. The saved are comforted as they await the resurrection of their new immortal bodies. The unsaved are in torment as they await their final judgment. Regarding the estate of the saved, the Apostle Paul wrote: "We are confident, I say, and willing rather to be absent from the body, and to be present with the Lord" (2 Corinthians 5:8).

While of the unsaved, we read: "And in hell he lift up his eyes, being in torments" (Luke 16:23).

How foolish for anyone to assume that the dead have no feeling or awareness of their existence. How foolish the comments that we often hear at funerals: "Now he is at peace," or "Now he will know no pain or sorrow." Such words cannot apply to the unsaved. They are in hell!

That is why I implore all who read this to recognize that "Ye are gods." We are eternal creatures made in the image and likeness of God. We are the offspring of the Most High. We are spirit beings who must someday give account! "Then shall the dust return to the earth as it was: and the spirit shall return unto God who gave it" (Ecclesiastes 12:7).

All of our efforts, therefore, should be directed toward objectives that have eternal value. First we need a right relationship with God the Father. This occurs when we are born again into the family of God through faith in God the Son. Finally, for the rest of our mortal lives, we need to achieve, practice, and maintain a right relationship with God the Holy Spirit. We need to obediently surrender our bodies for His use. We must confess with our mouths Jesus as Lord and use our talents and the gifts of the Holy Spirit to the glory of God until the day we are called home.

Yes, we are all gods, but we are not all Godlike. We all possess an eternal spirit, but the born again are, additionally, the temples of the Holy Spirit of God. We who have been redeemed are born from above. Even in this life we are members of the holy eternal family of God, and we bear His name. Thus the Apostle Paul could say: "For to me to live is Christ, and to die is gain" (Philippians 1:21).

We are the light of this sin-darkened world and the only hope this world has until the end of the church age. It is the Father's holy will that we, even in these frail, vile, mortal bodies, should live to His glory until our earthly journey is complete. "But we have this treasure [the light of the gospel] in earthen vessels, that the excellency of the power may be of God and not of us" (2 Corinthians 4:7).

And then, someday soon, we shall truly be like Him. In addition to His Spirit, we shall receive new and glorified bodies like His own! We shall be immortal at last and joint heirs with Jesus of all that God has planned for His chosen family from the foundation of the world. "Beloved, now are we the sons of God, and it doth not yet appear what we shall be: but we know that, when he shall appear, we shall be like him; for we shall see him as he is" (1 John 3:2).

This is the epitomy of God's answers to the mystery of life.

69

The Wrath of God

And I heard a great voice out of the temple saying to the seven angels, Go your ways, and pour out the vials of the wrath of God upon the earth.

Revelation 16:1

Thou shalt break them with a rod of iron; thou shalt dash them in pieces like a potter's vessel. . . . Serve the Lord with fear, and rejoice with trembling. Kiss the Son, lest he be angry, and ye perish from the way, when his wrath is kindled but a little.

Psalms 2:9-12

And the kings of the earth, and the great men, and the rich men, and the chief captains, and the mighty men, and every bondman, and every free man, hid themselves in the dens and in the rocks of the mountains; And said to the mountains and rocks, Fall on us, and hide us from the face of him that sitteth on the throne, and from the wrath of the Lamb.

Revelation 6:15, 16

Contemporary Christianity is great on the love of God, and rightly so, for God is love (*see* 1 John 4:8). However, we seem to have completely forgotten the wrath of God, and consequently, there seems to be no fear of God, either in the world or in the ranks of His holy church.

The world is content to believe that God is a grand old man up in the sky who commiserates with our human frailties and if we will only do our best, that's all He expects. The church for the most part seems content with the Scripture, "If we confess our sins, he is faithful and just to forgive us our sins, and to cleanse us from all unrighteousness" (1 John 1:9).

Whatever happened to hell? Whatever happened to the apostle's warning that "God is not mocked: for whatsoever a man soweth, that shall he also reap" (Galatians 6:7)? Or the Lord's admonition, "Why call ye me, Lord, Lord, and do not the things which I say?" (Luke 6:46).

Brethren, confession of sin is not enough, neither in the case of the unredeemed nor in respect to disobedient Christians! The unsaved are already condemned to hell and eternal death; their best works cannot save them. God has decreed that "All have sinned and come short of the glory of God" (Romans 8:23) and "except a man be born again, he cannot see the kingdom of God" (John 3:3). The nonchalant attitude of millions who ignore the Holy Scriptures will disappear at the final judgment, and they will confess too late that Jesus is Lord. Millions of the self-satisfied of this ignorant world will be resurrected from hell only to be cast into the lake of fire!

"And I saw the dead, small and great, stand before God . . . and whosoever was not found written in the book of life was cast into the lake of fire" (Revelation 20:12-15).

It is also true that there are many self-satisfied Christians who feel that because they are saved, they need not fear God. They are ignoring the many admonitions in the Word to live holy lives because someone has told them that when they were saved, all their sins—past, present, and future—were forgiven. Brethren, this is not scriptural. Sins have to be dealt with. *Confession to God includes repentance, restitution (when possible), and obedience to the known, holy will of God in every circumstance.* All sin must be brought under the sacred cleansing of the blood of Christ, or God must deal with it in His wrath!

"For we know him that hath said, Vengeance belongeth unto me, I will recompense, saith the Lord. And again, The Lord shall judge *his* people. It is a fearful thing to fall into the hands of the living God" (Hebrews 10:30, 31, italics added).

It is an experiential truth that the sins of Christians not only hurt their own lives and ruin their own testimonies, but also affect the lives of their children and their grandchildren. Listen to what God has said: "For I the Lord thy God am a jealous God, visiting the iniquity of the fathers upon the children [continuing to punish the children] unto the third and fourth generation of them that hate me" (Exodus 20:5).

The sins of Christian parents can cause their children to hate God and the church. This is a scriptural truth that we have all witnessed. Christian parents are all too often brokenhearted over sins in the family that have never been brought under the blood!

Now consider carefully the following verse: "For if we sin wilfully after that we have received the knowledge of the truth, there remaineth no more sacrifice for sins" (Hebrews 10:26).

Brethren, willful sinning is not automatically forgiven. When we were saved, we repented, and all our past sins were forgiven, but we must someday give account for our lives after we were saved. Repentance and restitution are ongoing requirements of the Christian walk. In regard to the foregoing Scripture, all Christian commentaries agree that the references to the "brethren" and to "us" in Hebrews 10:19-25 apply to the saved, but when they come to the "we" in verse 26, they assume it applies to the nearly saved. Verse 26 is either lifted out of its context or completely ignored.

Don't misunderstand this. The Bible clearly teaches that once we are truly saved, we are saved forever, but our willful sins of commission and omission after we are saved are not forgiven or forgotten until we get them under the blood. Unforgiven sin will be dealt with by God either during the course of our lives or at the judgment seat of Christ (*see* Romans 14:10).

I believe we should also be concerned about our sins of ignorance. (Sins we may not presently be aware of because we are so accustomed to unholy living!) We need to be more concerned because we have been commanded to live holy lives for the glory of God. "Because it is written, Be ye holy; for I am holy" (1 Peter 1:16).

This is why the Apostle Paul wrote: "work out your own salvation with fear and trembling" (Philippians 2:12).

Brethren, there is not much fear and trembling among Christians today. I wonder if they will still be so self-assured when they face God? For then all our sins will surely find us out (*see* Numbers 32:23) and every one of us shall give account of himself to God (*see* Romans 14:12). We won't lose our salvation at the judgment seat, but will we not experience a purging akin to purgatory? No defiled person can enter into the presence of a holy God, therefore our works (our life and our witness) must first be made manifest and tried by fire. "If any man's work shall be burned, he shall suffer loss: but he himself shall be saved; yet so as by fire" (1 Corinthians 3:15).

I'm not sure what this means. I doubt that we shall suffer physical pain as we are purged of unforgiven sin, but I am certain there will be a great deal of tearful repentance at the judgment seat of the Lamb!

Significantly, there are ten days from the Feast of Trumpets to the Day of Atonement as described in the Old Testament. These ten days were to be spent in prayer, fasting, and repentance in preparation for that day when the high priest went alone into the holiest place. Many Christian Hebrew scholars find a parallel here to the time between the last trump, when we are caught up to meet Him in the air, and the time we actually enter our heavenly home. Will we too spend ten days at the judgment seat?

Brethren, we know that the children of God will never experience the wrath of God in the same manner that it will be poured out on the wicked of this world in the last days. However, we will be made acutely aware of the horrible consequences of sin in the lives of all mankind. It is my point of view that we ought to be more concerned now!

70

Shaping Up for the Great Ecumenical Church

This know also, that in the last days perilous times shall come. For men shall be lovers of their own selves, covetous, boasters, proud, blasphemers, disobedient to parents, unthankful, unholy, Without natural affection, trucebreakers, false accusers, incontinent, fierce, despisers of those that are good, Traitors, heady, highminded, lovers of pleasures more than lovers of God; Having a form of godliness, but denying the power thereof: from such turn away.

2 Timothy 3:1-5

There are more professing Christians in the world today than ever before in the history of the Lord's church. However, like the seventh church of the Revelation, we are fast becoming lukewarm. Apostasy, the greatest weapon of Satan, is causing the falling away predicted by the Apostle Paul (*see* 2 Thessalonians 2:3), when the antichrist will be revealed. He will support and use this worldwide powerless church for his own purposes. This will be the great ecumenical church that many church leaders are espousing today. This church (the whore of Babylon, Revelation 17) will remain after the Lord has spued it from His mouth (*see* Revelation 3:16) and has taken a remnant of true believers to be with Him in heaven. It is my point of view that those raptured won't even be missed. In fact, they will be glad to be rid of us! However, this great ecumenical body will not last long, for the antichrist (the beast) will soon tire of her when her usefulness is past.

"And the ten horns which thou sawest upon the beast, these shall hate the whore, and shall make her desolate and naked, and shall eat her flesh, and burn her with fire" (Revelation 17:16).

It is alarming to note that the world and even the church is "shaping up" for these climatic events. Even those who call themselves evangelical are falling away from the truths of the Holy Word of God.

Have you noticed that hell is seldom mentioned in sermons anymore? When it becomes necessary for some sort of reference to the final abode of the unsaved, many preachers now refer to a "Christless eternity." This doesn't sound so bad, does it? Certainly it is much more palatable to the world than such words as *hell* and the *lake of fire*.

Whatever happened to words like *pervert, whore, whoremonger,* *sadist, sodomy* and phrases such as *living in sin?* These have been replaced by much more acceptable terms, such as *having a relationship, sexual preference, alternate life-style* and *gay.* Sad to relate, even the churches are using this language. And they are actually debating the authority of the Word of God regarding these matters and considering whether or not such practices should any longer be condemned. Would you believe that "gay rights" are now being equated with human rights? And we who believe otherwise are in the minority! Forgotten are the admonitions of the apostles:

> I wrote unto you in an epistle not to company with fornicators.
>
> 1 Corinthians 5:9

> Know ye not that the unrighteous shall not inherit the kingdom of God? Be not deceived: neither fornicators, nor idolators, nor adulterers, nor effeminate, nor abusers of themselves with mankind, Nor thieves, nor covetous, nor drunkards, nor revilers, nor extortioners, shall inherit the kingdom of God.
>
> 1 Corinthians 6:9, 10

> Dearly beloved, I beseech you as strangers and pilgrims, abstain from fleshly lusts which war against the soul.
>
> 1 Peter 2:11

Even the murder of unborn children is condoned in the world today, and the church of Jesus Christ is hardly lifting up her voice against it! One and one-half million children (it is less painful to call them fetuses) are killed annually in the United States alone. I don't see how God can withhold His wrath much longer! Brethren, the

Bible makes it crystal clear that every unborn child is a living creation of God. "Before I formed thee in the belly I knew thee; and before thou camest forth out of the womb I sanctified thee" (Jeremiah 1:5). How dare we destroy that child's right to live?

John the Baptist prepared the way of the Lord by preaching repentance. His baptism was the baptism of repentance. When the Apostle Peter preached his very first sermon and his hearers asked, "What must we do to be saved?" Peter's reply was "repent and be baptized." Yet repentance is seldom mentioned in the gospel of today's churches. All one need do is "come to Jesus" or "believe in Jesus" and "He will receive you just as you are."

We are told that "His grace is greater than all our sins," and "Smile, God loves you." True, but there is still the necessity of genuine repentance. We can easily join a local church merely by coming forward and by a childlike confession of faith, and all confessors are most heartily welcomed in the ecumenical body, *but we are not saved if we will not turn from our sins!* Being a Christian and living the Christian life is not easy. It is a life of continual conviction, repentance, and sacrifice. Churches that promulgate a gospel of easy grace, health, wealth, and happiness are of their father, the devil.

I have learned that the longer I walk with Jesus and the closer I walk with Him, the more I recognize my inherent human weakness and sinfulness. I am unworthy of the blessings God provides. I have also learned that inner peace and joy are not contingent upon blessings. They emanate from the confidence of knowing *Whose I am!* We who are truly the Lord's have a joy the world can never match or understand, but we are not always smiling. Sometimes we hurt.

Then there is the matter of tithes and offerings. This is seldom mentioned anymore, as it offends the majority of churchgoers. However, the Scriptures plainly state that the tithe—10 percent—is the Lord's. We cannot give a tithe; we cannot give that which is rightfully His. Only when we return to the Lord a portion over and above His tithe can we call it an offering or a gift. Actually, all that we have is given to us by God, so how can we give Him anything? We are called to be good stewards of all that God has given us.

Some have argued that we in the church age are not under the law, therefore the tithe does not apply. Neither was our father Abraham under the law, but he recognized the tithe as the Lord's portion (*see* Genesis 14:20). Christians today generally give God some of what is leftover after they pay their bills, deposit their savings, and set aside their needs for eating, pleasure, and entertaining. Very few tithe or give sacrificially, and fasting is out! Our missionaries are forced to live at the poverty level, and we are not ashamed. *Consequently, our Lord's command to make disciples of all nations is for the most part failing because Christians are not willing to give of themselves or their possessions for His sake.*

I am reminded that the first Christians gave all that they had for the apostles' use. "And all that believed were together, and had all things common; And sold their possessions and goods, and parted them to all men, as every man had need" (Acts 2:44, 45).

God never has demanded our all. These early Christians gave because they wanted to. It really makes me squirm in a worship service when we sing that popular hymn, "I Surrender All." It's a wonder they don't have to drag us all out by the feet and bury us, as they did Ananias and Sapphira (*see* Acts 5:1-11).

Finally, Christians were meant to be light and salt to a lost world. This requires much more than living a good life and doing good works. Jesus said, "Let your light so shine before men, that they may see your good works, and glorify your Father which is in heaven" (Matthew 5:16).

Much of the good works being performed in our society today are being done by folks who are not Christians. Many good citizens are doing much more than Christians are doing. Needless to say, God is not glorified in most of these worthwhile endeavors. He is not glorified in the current battle for "human rights." He is not even mentioned.

So how do we make our light so shine? It is my point of view that God is glorified when our good works are performed humbly, even secretly, and are accompanied by our Christian witness. God is not glorified by silent Christians. We must "confess with thy mouth the Lord Jesus" (Romans 10:9). Our light is the Word of God hidden in our hearts and spoken with our mouths. "Thy word have I hid in mine heart, that I might not sin against thee" (Psalms 119:11).

"Thy word is a lamp unto my feet, and a light unto my path" (Psalms 119:105).

Silent Christians are neither light nor salt. Being the salt of the earth implies getting involved! *We need to make an impact for God wherever we are and whatever we do.* We all have talents and spiritual gifts that are to be used to glorify our Lord. Going to church is not enough. The Christian *is* the church, wherever he goes. Each of us has an important part in the body of Christ. We need to ask ourselves, "Am I functioning or useless?"

"Ye are the salt of the earth: but if the salt have lost his savour, wherewith shall it be salted? it is thenceforth good for nothing, but to be cast out, and to be trodden under foot of men" (Matthew 5:13).

Brethren, I'm afraid that the church is fast falling away from all that God requires. If there is no revival in the hearts of His people soon, we will become the lukewarm church of the last days!

71
The Will of God

Father, if thou be willing, remove this cup from me: nevertheless not my will, but thine, be done.

Luke 22:42

The will of God is one of the most important subjects and perhaps the least understood in all of God's Holy Word. If God the Son so labored in prayer to God the Father, we had better pay attention. Jesus certainly knew the will of the Father in regard to His coming sacrificial suffering, so we may assume that His plea was uttered and recorded for the edification and profit of His disciples, and that includes us.

All too often we hear Christians utter this: "It was God's will." We hear it repeatedly after some of the most tragic experiences and disappointments. It is a common panacea for all our misfortunes and ills. All too often we have prayed, seemingly in vain, and then we have given up because God has not answered our prayers as we had hoped.

Brethren, it is not God's *holy* will that any should suffer, not even His only begotten Son. But there are circumstances when, by His *permissive* will, He must allow suffering in order to accomplish His eternal plans. Yes, God is in charge, and nothing occurs without His prior awareness and permission. *But we must learn to recognize the distinction between God's holy will and His permissive will.*

When we suffer, God suffers, too. He cried over the city of Jerusalem. It was His holy will that all Jerusalem should be saved and ultimately become the greatest city in all the world, but in His permissive will God knew that the wicked, unbelieving, and unrepentant in Israel must first be destroyed for the sake of future believers and the ultimate glory of Jerusalem.

"O Jerusalem, Jerusalem, thou that killest the prophets, and stonest them which are sent unto thee, how often would I have gathered thy children together, even as a hen gathereth her chickens under her wings, and ye would not!" (Matthew 23:37).

Jesus wept at the tomb of Lazarus. It was not His holy will that His loved ones should suffer so. But by His permissive will, He allowed the death of Lazarus so God might be glorified and many of His unbelieving brethren might be saved. "Jesus saith unto her [Martha], Said I not unto thee, that, if thou wouldest believe, thou shouldest see the glory of God?" (John 11:40).

"Then many of the Jews which came to Mary, and had seen the things which Jesus did, believed on him" (John 11:45).

Even Satan is allowed to live for a predestined time and purpose by God's permissive will. Certainly it was not God's holy will to create the evil one and to inflict misery on all His creation. But an all-wise Father knew what sin can and would do. He knew that He could not force all mankind to love and obey Him. He knew He must separate the wheat from the chaff. He knew He must patiently wait for all His chosen ones to be born and saved. And when all those names written in the Lamb's book of life are safely in the fold, He will deal with Satan and his followers once and for all! God's holy will for all eternity will be accomplished at last.

Those of us who are hurting and feel that our prayers for help and healing have not been answered should recognize that our condition is not His holy will. He understands. He grieves with us. Our pain is also His pain. And He doesn't want us to resign our fate to the "will of God" and give up. We need to keep on praying, and we have the right to ask, "Why?" We should know that there is a purpose to everything God allows. "And we know that all things work together for good to them that love God" (Romans 8:28).

Now I am not one of those dummies who say "Thank You, Lord" for everything bad that happens to me. I believe God expects me to ask, "Why, Lord?" and to pray about it.

Maybe, like the Apostle Paul, we need to recognize our infirmities as opportunities to glorify God. We should recognize that our friends, our neighbors, and our loved ones are watching. *We need to show them how a Christian handles it.* We need to demonstrate our faith before them. We need to believe always that God can and will heal us if and when it is the very best thing for us and for our Christian witness. Meanwhile, we should pray that the beauty of Jesus might be seen in us, regardless.

Maybe many of our loved ones and friends will learn to believe on Jesus because of our faith in what God can and will do. We may or may not experience a miraculous deliverance, but we, like our blessed Savior, must learn to pray, "nevertheless not my will, but thine, be done."

72

Israel

For thou art an holy people unto the LORD thy God: the LORD thy God hath chosen thee to be a special people unto himself, above all people that are upon the face of the earth.

Deuteronomy 7:6

Make no mistake about it: the Israelis are God's chosen people. The world may hate the Jews, but God has chosen them above all the nations of the world, and they will yet serve Him and bring glory to His name!

"Blessed is the nation whose God is the LORD; and the people whom he hath chosen for his own inheritance" (Psalms 33:12).

"Hear, O Israel: the LORD our God is one LORD" (Deuteronomy 6:4).

Israel's most glorious years were during the reigns of kings David and Solomon, but even then the nation did not give God the glory due Him, nor were they an effective witness to the pagan nations around them. Eventually, they turned from the Holy Word of God that had been entrusted to them and became worshipers of idols and evil deities. It is difficult to understand how a people such as they, who had been given so many signs and miraculous deliverances, could turn from worshiping the true and only God, but they did. I think the lesson we can learn from their experience is that faith doesn't come by signs and wonders.

Faith comes and grows when we trust God, learn obedience, and prove Him by the works we do as we strive to live to His glory. If our objectives and the experiences of our daily lives do not bring glory to His name, He will most surely chastise us, even as He has His beloved Israel. "For whom the Lord loveth he chasteneth" (Hebrews 12:6).

God allowed Israel to fall into captivity. The ten northern tribes were captured by the Assyrians in approximately 720 B.C. The southern kingdom (Judah and Benjamin) were taken captive to

Babylon in 600 B.C. During their captivity, the northern tribes completely lost their identity and never returned. Judah, however, was predestined by the Lord to return in fulfillment of Jacob's ancient prophecy: "The sceptre shall not depart from Judah, nor a lawgiver from between his feet, until Shiloh [the Prince of Peace] come; and unto him shall the gathering of the people be" (Genesis 49:10).

Some five hundred years before the birth of our Lord, a small remnant of the tribes of Judah, Benjamin, and the Levites returned to their homeland to rebuild the temple and the walls of Jerusalem, as recorded in the books of Ezra and Nehemiah. However, Israel has never regained her former glory. Only Judah retained her identity and gave birth to those descendants of David who would bring forth Jesus, the Savior of the world. They reoccupied only a small portion of the land that God had given to Abraham, Isaac, and Jacob. It was called the land of Judaea, and the people were called Jews.

The Jewish people were still not a nation. They endured humiliating serfdom under the successive rulership of Persia, Greece, and Syria, when in 170 B.C. Antiochus Epiphanes plundered Jerusalem and profaned the temple. This brought about the revolt of the heroic Maccabees, a godly band of Jews who determined to free the nation. They did, for a while, regain possession of Jerusalem and purified and rededicated the temple. Their successors, however, were not so virtuous. They established a line of priest-rulers for the land of Judaea, and a civil war followed. Their rule was quickly terminated by the Romans. Julius Caesar appointed Herod king of the Jews in 40 B.C.

This was the condition of the ragtag nation of Israel when God fulfilled His Old Testament promises to send them the Messiah.

"Therefore the Lord himself shall give you a sign; Behold, a virgin shall conceive, and bear a son, and shall call his name Immanuel" (Isaiah 7:14).

"For unto us a child is born, unto us a son is given: and the government shall be upon his shoulder: and his name shall be called Wonderful, Counsellor, The mighty God, The everlasting Father, The Prince of Peace" (Isaiah 9:6).

The time, place, and exacting conditions of the first appearance of Israel's Messiah are all given in the Old Testament. Jesus Christ fulfilled every written prophecy concerning His first advent in exact detail. His unique birth, His life, His deeds, His death, and His resurrection were all vividly predicted by Israel's prophets. But Israel, because of her sinfulness, her blindness to the sure Word of God, her undeserving expectation of immediate rescue from the yoke of Rome, and in anticipation only of the glory that God had promised them, failed to recognize that Messiah must first suffer and die—not only for Israel but potentially for the sins of the whole world. "All we like sheep have gone astray; we have turned every one to his own way; and the LORD hath laid on him the iniquity of us all" (Isaiah 53:6).

"He came unto his own [Israel], and his own received him not. But as many as received him [individual Jews and Gentiles], to them gave he power to become the sons of God" (John 1:11, 12).

And so the church of Jesus Christ (a mystery to Israel) was born. We are commanded to disciple all nations (*see*Matthew 28:19), beginning at Jerusalem. We are God's present-day ambassadors to reveal the good news (the Gospel) that whosoever will accept the Messiah of Israel shall be saved!

Meanwhile, Israel is again set aside by God. They, as a nation, cannot be used in their unbelief. In A.D. 70 the Romans destroyed their temple and their holy city and drove them to the far corners of the earth. They have been strangers in other lands for 1900 years, but God has not forgotten them. "I say then, Hath God cast away his people? God forbid ... God hath not cast away his people which he foreknew" (Romans 11:1, 2).

By His foreknowledge God knows that Israel will repent, and He knows exactly when. God will regather His people and return them to their own land, as He has promised. "But, The LORD liveth, which brought up and which led the seed of the house of Israel out of the north country, and from all countries whither I had driven them; and they shall dwell in their own land" (Jeremiah 23:8).

"Therefore the redeemed of the LORD shall return, and come with singing unto Zion; and everlasting joy shall be upon their head" (Isaiah 51:11).

At 12:01 A.M., May 15, 1948, Israel was reborn. A long-dead nation had come back to life. There was dancing in the streets. Despite the fierce opposition of her Arab neighbors, who determined to drive her into the sea, Israel is again a nation. They now boast one of the strongest, though tiniest, military forces in all the world. Their scientific and technical knowledge is second to none, and they are showing the world how to bring to new life a long-neglected and barren land. Indeed, as the ancient prophets have foretold, the desert is blooming! Water drawn from the Sea of Galilee and the Jordan River gives life to citrus, vegetables, vineyards, and date and fig trees. More than 100 million trees of all kinds now cover the once-barren hills, and they are actually importing wild animals to populate these new forests.

As in Nehemiah's time, they work with a will, with a weapon in one hand. These first-generation Israelis have accomplished miracles of rebuilding their cities while fighting five wars and suffering through innumerable terrorist attacks. They are, and will continue to be, invincible, simply because their time has come and Almighty God is on their side!

It is my point of view that because Israel, at last, is back in the land of promise, the end of "the times of the Gentiles" is very near. "And they [Israel] shall fall by the edge of the sword, and shall be led away captive into all nations: and Jerusalem shall be trodden down of the Gentiles, until the times of the Gentiles be fulfilled" (Luke 21:24).

Israel is now firmly entrenched in its own land. They rule Jerusalem and the entire West Bank, which they shall never relinquish again.

The time and work of the church is nearly over. I believe they are already falling away and the Lord will call them home very soon.

Then will come the time of Jacob's trouble (*see*Jeremiah 30:7) or the Great Tribulation, when Israel shall suffer her greatest persecution under the reign of the Beast (*see*Revelation 13). He will pretend to be the friend of Israel, and the nation will be deceived for the last time. Their blindness shall be taken away, and with great repentance they will recognize at last that our Lord Jesus is their Messiah!

A remnant (one-third) of the nation of Israel will survive the horrors of the Great Tribulation. God will hear their cry for deliverance and save them.

And it shall come to pass in that day, that I will seek to destroy all the nations that come against Jerusalem. And I will pour upon the house of David, and upon the inhabitants of Jerusalem, the spirit of grace and of supplications: and they shall look upon me whom they have pierced, and they shall mourn for him, as one mourneth for his only son.

Zechariah 12:9, 10

"And one shall say unto him, What are these wounds in thine hands? Then he shall answer, Those with which I was wounded in the house of my friends" (Zechariah 13:6).

"And I will bring the third part through the fire, and will refine them as silver is refined, and will try them as gold is tried: they shall call on my name, and I will hear them: I will say, It is my people: and they shall say, The LORD is my God" (Zechariah 13:9).

The LORD will return in great glory to save His people and utterly destroy the Beast and his armies. Jesus will then reign for a thousand years from the throne of David in Jerusalem. Israel will be the greatest and most powerful nation in the world, and Jerusalem will be the capital of all nations. The Word of the LORD shall go forth from Israel in the greatest missionary movement this world has ever known. Israel will witness to the world that Jesus is LORD. They will glorify God, as He knew they would when He first chose them. Israel will be a blessing to all the peoples of the earth.

"And the remnant of Jacob shall be in the midst of many people as a dew from the LORD" (Micah 5:7).

"For out of Zion shall go forth the law, and the word of the LORD from Jerusalem" (Isaiah 2:3).

"Arise, shine; for thy light is come, and the glory of the LORD is risen upon thee [Israel] . . . And the Gentiles shall come to thy light, and kings to the brightness of thy rising" (Isaiah 60:1, 3).

The twelve tribes shall be completely restored and shall possess all the land that God has promised them "from the river of Egypt unto the great river, the river Euphrates" (Genesis 15:18).

"Thus saith the Lord God; This shall be the border, whereby ye shall inherit the land according to the twelve tribes of Israel" (Ezekiel 47:13).

And so Israel will fulfill her destiny at last. It is they who will preach the Gospel of the kingdom to all nations. It is they who will serve the Lion of Judah when He reigns and rules with a rod of iron from Mt. Zion.

"And he said, It is a light thing that thou shouldest be my servant to raise up the tribes of Jacob, and to restore the preserved of Israel:

I will also give thee for a light to the Gentiles, that thou mayest be my salvation unto the end of the earth" (Isaiah 49:6).

Israel will glorify God, and in turn will be glorified before all the nations.

"In those days it shall come to pass, that ten men shall take hold out of all languages of the nations, even shall take hold of the skirt of him that is a Jew, saying, We will go with you: for we have heard that God is with you" (Zechariah 8:23).

The Jews will then be missionaries to the Gentiles, even as Jesus had explained to His disciples: "And this gospel of the kingdom [when Christ shall reign] shall be preached in all the world for a witness unto all nations; and then shall the end come" (Matthew 24:14).

The disciples asked, "What shall be the sign of thy coming, and of the end of the world?" (Matthew 24:3). The Lord's detailed reply in Matthew 24 has nothing to do with the church. The above verse is too often quoted completely out of context in this respect. Jesus was describing the time of the Great Tribulation for Israel after the church has been caught up into heaven. Jesus was talking about His second coming in power and great glory, His judgment of the nations, His earthly rule, and ultimately, the end of the world. It is Israel who will preach the Gospel of the kingdom to all nations. It is Israel who will complete the task that the church was originally commissioned to do. The Lord knew this from the beginning. He knew the potential of His chosen people.

During the thousand-year reign of our Lord in Israel, the nations of the world will be compelled to send their ambassadors to the glorious nation, "For the nation and kingdom that will not serve thee shall perish" (Isaiah 60:12).

So when we pray, "Thy kingdom come, thy will be done on earth," we should recognize we are praying for the kingdom of David and Israel! For God has made an eternal covenant with them.

"Once have I sworn by my holiness that I will not lie unto David. His seed shall endure for ever, and his throne as the sun before me" (Psalms 89:35, 36).

"Thou hast kept me to be head of the heathen: a people which I knew not shall serve me [David]" (2 Samuel 22:44).

"They shall serve the LORD their God, and David their king, whom I will raise up unto them" (Jeremiah 30:9).

"And the Lord God shall give unto him [Jesus] the throne of his father David" (Luke 1:32).

After a thousand years of peace on earth under the authoritative rule of Christ, Satan will be loosed for a little while (*see* Revelation 20:7). He will deceive the nations again, and the unredeemed of this world will make war against the Lord and His beloved kingdom of Israel. This will be the last war! All of the lost will be slain, resurrected, judged, and finally cast into the lake of fire with Satan. This earth and the heavens that we know will be utterly destroyed.

God will then reveal new heavens and a new earth especially prepared for all His saints to know and enjoy for all eternity. We don't know what part Israel will play in the new earth, but we do know for certain that her glory is about to be revealed on this present wicked planet!

This means the rapture of the Lord's church must be very near. We ought to be living as though Jesus might call us out today! As Enoch was caught up before the flood, even so will the church be caught up before the Great Tribulation. Even so, come Lord Jesus.

In conclusion, may I add that this is certainly not meant to be a comprehensive overview of Israel. It is intended only to emphasize a few apparently forgotten truths from God's Word regarding His chosen nation. I am appalled at the lack of comprehension in the church today regarding our relationship to these beloved people. Brethren, Israel is likened to a holy olive tree chosen of God to bring forth fruit for His glory. True, many of the branches were broken off because of their unbelief, and we, the church (the wild olive tree) were fortunate to be grafted in. But we have nothing to be high-minded about. Many Gentile professors are also being broken off, for they bear no fruit whatsoever.

As the Apostle Paul has written, we need to remember our place:

And if some of the [natural] branches be broken off, and thou, being a wild olive tree, wert graffed [grafted] in among them, and with them partakest of the root and fatness of the olive tree; Boast not against the branches. But if thou boast, [then bear in mind] thou bearest not the root, but the root thee.

Romans 11:17, 18

Israel is God's provision to bring forth to the world the written Word and the Living Word, *God's answers to the mystery of life.*

73
Abortion Is Murder!

Deliver me from bloodguiltiness, O God.

Psalms 51:14

All human life is sacred to God, and the shedding of human blood is forbidden by the statutes of God. "For the life of the flesh is in the blood" (Leviticus 17:11). When the sperm of the human male fertilizes an egg of a human female, *if God wills,* life is created. We must never forget this truth: God is the Creator. Our lives are not by chance! "The Spirit of God hath made me, and the breath of the Almighty hath given me life" (Job 33:4).

When a new life is created, it is neither the father's life nor the mother's life. It is a whole new identity, and the blood in that new person is neither the blood of the mother nor the father. The blood is the life of the flesh of a new creation, and that life and that blood are sacred to God.

The Israelites under the Law of the Covenant were forbidden to eat the meat of any animal that was not thoroughly drained of all blood. "For it [the blood] is the life of all flesh . . . whosoever eateth it shall be cut off" (Leviticus 17:14).

Furthermore, the shedding of human blood is the most serious violation of all the laws of God, for He has said, "Thou shalt not kill." And if we deliberately take a human life, we deserve to die, too. "Whoso sheddeth man's blood, by man shall his blood be shed: for in the image of God made he man" (Genesis 9:6).

Brethren, God's laws have never been repealed! Jesus said, "Think not that I am come to destroy the law, or the prophets: I am not come to destroy, but to fulfil. For verily I say unto you, Till heaven and earth pass, one jot or one tittle shall in no wise pass from the law" (Matthew 5:17, 18).

All human life is sacred. Man is not just another animal; we were made in the image of God! We have an eternal spirit, given to us by God when He formed us in our mother's womb. That spirit must

209

someday return and give account to God. That spirit will someday be clothed with a new body fitted either for destruction or for eternal life with God. That new life formed in our mother's womb is not just a fetus. It is a new, unique creation formed by God *for an eternal purpose!*.

> For thou hast possessed my reins [formed my inner components]: thou has covered [fashioned] me in my mother's womb. I will praise thee; for I am fearfully and wonderfully made: marvelous are thy works; and that my soul knoweth right well. My substance was not hid from thee, when I was made in secret, and curiously wrought in the lowest parts of the earth. Thine eyes did see my substance, yet being unperfect; and in thy book all my members were written, which in continuance were fashioned, when as yet there was none of them.
>
> Psalms 139:13-16

David wrote that God formed him in his mother's womb, and the eyes of God saw him as he would be, though his substance as yet had no form. God planned all his days before he was born.

Now hear the Word of the Lord as He spoke to His prophet Jeremiah: "Before I formed thee in the belly I knew thee; and before thou camest forth out of the womb I sanctified thee, and I ordained thee a prophet unto the nations" (Jeremiah 1:5).

Jeremiah was known by God before he was even conceived. He was sanctified and ordained while he was yet in his mother's womb, and so are all of God's elect.

Who has the right to terminate the life of any unborn child? How are we to know what they might become?

The fruit of the womb in the Bible was always considered a new and precious human life. It was as priceless to its parents while in the womb as it ever would be. It was cherished and protected by its parents and by the laws of God. If the unborn child or the mother was hurt or killed, even by accident, the offender was punished accordingly.

> If men strive, and hurt a woman with child, so that her fruit depart from her, and yet no mischief [lasting harm] follow: he shall be surely punished, accordingly as the woman's

husband will lay upon him; and he shall pay as the judges determine. And if any mischief follow, then thou shalt give life for life, Eye for eye, tooth for tooth.

Exodus 21: 22-24

The deliberate murder of one's own child was most certainly never contemplated by the mothers of God's chosen people. Such a crime was unthinkable!

One of the most beautiful illustrations of the unique awareness of life of the unborn child is provided in the exciting experiences of Jesus' mother, Mary, and her cousin Elizabeth. Mary had just been told by the angel Gabriel that she would "conceive in thy womb, and bring forth a son, and shalt call his name Jesus" (Luke 1:31). The Holy Spirit then came upon her and she was made pregnant. We don't know how many days passed after this, but the Scriptures record that Mary went into the hill country with haste to see and tell Elizabeth, who was already six months pregnant with John the Baptist. The account of John's awareness of Jesus is chronicled for our edification.

And it came to pass, that, when Elizabeth heard the salutation of Mary, the babe leaped in her womb; and Elizabeth was filled with the Holy Ghost: And she spake out with a loud voice, and said, Blessed art thou among women, and blessed is the fruit of thy womb. And whence is this to me, that the mother of my Lord should come to me? For, lo, as soon as the voice of thy salutation sounded in mine ears, the babe leaped in my womb for joy.

Luke 1:41-44

Every woman in Israel considered herself blessed of the Lord when the conception of a new life occurred within her body. A married woman who was barren felt that the Lord was displeased for some reason. The wife would take the matter to God in contrite prayer. Therefore, both Elizabeth and Mary felt blessed of God for the life in their wombs.

But Elizabeth felt even more blessed in the presence of Mary. The Holy Spirit revealed to her that the new life in Mary was the Son of God. The Scriptures make it unmistakenly evident that the new life within Mary was not just a senseless fetus.

I believe both John and Jesus were new, living creations of God, and that this is true of all children at the moment of conception. I believe they were also to some degree aware of their existence, and perhaps even their ultimate purpose for living, while they were yet in the womb. Otherwise, why would the Scriptures relate that John leaped for joy? At what point in time the human embryo is first aware of its own existence, we just don't know. Nevertheless, the unborn child is a living human, and to deliberately destroy that life is an act of murder!

74

Christian Denominations

And for their sakes I sanctify myself, that they also might be sanctified through the truth. Neither pray I for these alone, but for them also which shall believe on me through their word; That they all may be one; as thou, Father, art in me, and I in thee, that they also may be one in us: that the world may believe that thou has sent me.

John 17:19-21

One of the reasons that the Lord's church is making so little impact in the world these days is the divisions among us. Jesus prayed that we would be one with the Father and with Him, so that the world might believe. This was the condition of the early church when it was said of them, "These that have turned the world upside down" (Acts 17:6). There was power in their unity. The church today is hopelessly divided, and our creditability and witness to an unbelieving world suffers.

Sometimes I think the religions of the world and the divisions in the Christian religion are Satan's favorite weapons. He uses them to separate the people of the world from God and Christians from one another. False teaching, the lies of Satan, and the philosophies of men have blinded the minds of mankind from the beginning.

What more could God have done? He gave man His holy written Word, and He proved it all by becoming the Living Word fulfilled through Jesus Christ, our Lord. Even as the Apostle John has written:

That which was from the beginning, which we have heard, which we have seen with our eyes, which we have looked upon, and our hands have handled, of the Word of life . . . That which we have seen and heard declare we unto you, that ye also may have fellowship with us: and truly our fellowship is with the Father, and with His Son Jesus Christ.

And these things write we unto you, that your joy may be full.

1 John 1:1, 3, 4

Brethren, we are called to fellowship around the Word of God. If we are all prayerfully reading the same sacred book and the Holy Spirit of God is our interpreter, there should be no divisions among us. Shame on those who are so proud of their own opinions, their independence, and their separation from their brothers and sisters in Christ!

Certainly, there will be differences in comprehension, in wisdom, and in spiritual growth, but as the Apostle Paul has cautioned us, these are no excuse for doubtful disputations (*see*Romans 14:1).

One may believe that he should refrain from eating certain foods, from drinking any form of alcohol, or from certain practices. One may observe certain holy days and practice prayer and fasting more than his fellows. Some enjoy an emotional worship experience, while others prefer a more sedate atmosphere. We need to recognize that we come from varying cultures and backgrounds that mold our character, but again, as the Apostle Paul has cautioned us, these things must not divide us. It's a matter between us and the Lord to be all that we believe God wants us to be. Paul wrote, "Let every man be fully persuaded in his own mind" (Romans 14:5).

A newborn Christian doesn't have the same amount of faith or the same convictions as an older saint, and he may never have them. What we practice is a matter of faith between each individual and the Lord. "I know, and am persuaded by the Lord Jesus, that there is nothing unclean of itself: but to him that esteemeth any thing to be unclean, to him it is unclean" (Romans 14:14).

This same attitude should prevail in regard to interpretations of prophecy and doctrine. None of us understand it all, and none of us can be certain that all our opinions are true. "For now we see through a glass, darkly," and we know only in part" (1 Corinthians 13:12), but someday, praise God, we shall know even as we are known. The *fundamentals of our salvation* are so clear that even a little child can understand them. The things that we do not fully understand should never divide us.

We are reminded by the apostle also that the Holy Spirit gives different gifts to the children of God. Some have greater spiritual insight than others and are called to be teachers; some are more equipped to be pastors or evangelists; some are given to ministries of comfort and healing; and all of us are called to be helps. But we are all members of the same body, and our ministry gifts are to be tempered by our love for God and our love for one another (1 Corinthians 12, 13).

"By this shall all men know that ye are my disciples, if ye have love one to another" (John 13:35).

So many of our variant beliefs are derived from the doctrines of assumedly brilliant Christian writers. Maybe we ought to quit reading so many books and look again to the Bible for our answers. It is my point of view that God's Word contains all the answers to our problems and the differences that confound us. And finally, with a "decent respect to the opinions of mankind," may I declare unto you, that as far as God is concerned, *there is only one church.* It consists of all who have not only accepted Christ as their Savior, but by their obedience have made Him their Lord! I believe there will be a lot of surprises in heaven among all Christian denominations when we see who our brothers and sisters really are.

75

Cockeyed Theology

Whom having not seen, ye love; in whom, though now ye see him not, yet believing, ye rejoice with joy unspeakable and full of glory.

1 Peter 1:8

I am annoyed at the current de-emphasis on feelings in evangelical preaching and writing. "Don't depend on your feelings to know you are saved," is heard a little too often, and I'm afraid it is misleading many recent converts. It's true that our emotions cannot save us, nor are they, alone, dependable criteria regarding the veracity of salvation. We are saved by the grace of God and our faith in the sacrifice of Jesus, our Savior and our Lord. But don't tell me that if you have truly been born again into the family of God you don't have to feel it. If you don't feel any different the day after you are saved, you must be dead as a doorknob!

"The joy of the hypocrite [is] but for a moment" (Job 20:5).

"These things have I spoken unto you, that my joy might remain in you, and that your joy might be full" (John 15:11).

If you suddenly inherited or won fifty million dollars, you would jump up and down for joy. And don't tell me you wouldn't feel anything the day after. Yet that is exactly what some theologians are telling those recently born again into life everlasting. Being saved from death and hell and becoming recipients of God's grace and inheriting all the promises of God, including heaven and the new earth, which shall last for all eternity, should be a lot more exciting than fifty million dollars. If it isn't you really haven't experienced the glory! "But as it is written, Eye hath not seen, nor ear heard, neither have entered into the heart of man, the things which God hath prepared for them that love him" (1 Corinthians 2:9).

"Whom [Jesus] having not seen, ye love; in whom, though now ye see him not, yet believing, ye rejoice with joy unspeakable and full of glory" (1 Peter 1:8).

How could anyone be rejoicing with joy unspeakable and full of God's glory without feeling it?

To me, the most thrilling evidence and the most compelling persuasion permeating my mind and my emotions is the fact that the Holy Spirit of God is now dwelling within me, making me a new creation. "And I will pray the Father, and he shall give you another Comforter, that he may abide with you for ever" (John 14:16).

"But ye are not in the flesh, but in the Spirit, if so be that the Spirit of God dwell in you. Now if any man have not the Spirit of Christ, he is none of his" (Romans 8:9).

"Therefore if any man be in Christ, he is a new creature" (2 Corinthians 5:17).

How could anyone with the Holy Spirit—the very presence of God—dwelling within him, not feel it? His Spirit becomes the guide, counselor, and conscience of every true believer.

And finally we know and feel the peace of God. We know that the very Creator of heaven and earth loves us and watches over us, His angels are guarding us, and we are securely in His care for all eternity, no matter what! "Peace I leave with you, my peace I give unto you: not as the world giveth, give I unto you. Let not your heart be troubled, neither let it be afraid" (John 14:27).

"Thou wilt keep him in perfect peace, whose mind is stayed on thee: because he trusteth in thee" (Isaiah 26:3).

"For I am persuaded, that neither death, nor life, nor angels, nor principalities, nor powers, nor things present, nor things to come, Nor height, nor depth, nor any other creature, shall be able to separate us from the love of God, which is in Christ Jesus our Lord" (Romans 8:38, 39).

So then, these feelings which the unsaved cannot experience, constantly reassure me that I am a child of God. To teach otherwise is cockeyed theology.

76

In Jesus' Name

And whatsoever ye shall ask in my name, that will I do, that the Father may be glorified in the son.

John 14:13

"Hitherto have ye asked nothing in my name: ask, and ye shall receive, that your joy may be full" (John 16:24). What did Jesus mean when He said we should pray in His name? The church today tacks these words onto the end of every prayer, as though they had some magical power! I believe our Lord had something greater in mind than the mere use of the words, "In Jesus' name."

Please note that He did not use these words in the model prayer that He taught His disciples (*see* Matthew 6:9-13). Nor is it recorded anywhere in the New Testament that His followers used these words as we do.

However, the apostles went out preaching and teaching and performing miracles in the power of Jesus' name! The first apostolic miracle, the healing of a lame man who was asking alms, is recorded as follows: "Then Peter said, Silver and gold have I none; but such as I have give I thee: In the name of Jesus Christ of Nazareth rise up and walk" (Acts 3:6).

Throughout their ministry, the apostles performed miracles of healing, casting out demons, and even raising the dead in the power of Jesus' name. They preached the Word and taught in the name of Jesus. They "turned the world upside down" so much that they were commanded by the authorities "not to speak at all nor teach in the name of Jesus" (Acts 4:18). This same power was not given to all of the Lord's followers, nor is it given to us today, but we are admonished, nevertheless, to continue the work in Jesus' name. "And whatsoever ye do in word or deed, do all in the name of the Lord Jesus, giving thanks to God and the Father by him" (Colossians 3:17).

I believe that when Jesus instructed His followers to pray in His name and to ask for things in His name, He meant that we are to represent Him. We are to pray to the Father as Christ would pray, and we are to pray that God's will might be done. Certainly, God cannot give us everything we ask for just because we use the words *in Jesus' name*. And we know that He doesn't! He is the Master Potter, and we are the clay. He is preparing us for eternity, and even the sore trials He allows are for our ultimate perfection.

The secret of the power and the success of our prayers is found in the following sacred verses: "And this is the confidence that we have in him, that, if we ask anything according to his will, he heareth us: And if we know that he hear us, whatsoever we ask, we know that we have the petitions that we desired of him" (1 John 5:14, 15).

When we pray that His will be done, we are praying as His advocates. And this, I believe, is praying in Jesus' name. However, we are challenged to know the mind of Christ so that whatsoever we ask is exactly what our Lord desires. "Let this mind be in you, which was also in Christ Jesus" (Philippians 2:5).

"For who hath known the mind of the Lord, that he may instruct him? But we have the mind of Christ" (1 Corinthians 2:16).

We can experience a triumphant prayer life when we have learned this wonderful truth. However, we don't know the mind of Christ in every matter, so we ask what we think is best and pray that, above all, His will might be done. We can then conclude our prayer with the confidence that God knows best and will answer our prayers accordingly.

In the Garden of Gethsemane, Jesus prayed, "Father, if thou be willing, remove this cup from me: nevertheless not my will, but thine, be done" (Luke 22:42). I believe our Lord's example best epitomizes the truth of all that it means to pray in Jesus' name.

In my own prayer life I shall continue to use the words *in Jesus' name* at the close of every prayer. However, I am much more cognizant now of their real and deeper meaning. My life must count for Him, and I must pray through Him and for Him to the glory of God the Father. I am Jesus' representative before all whose lives I touch. It is an awesome responsibility.

When I pray for friends and loved ones, I am vividly aware that I so often ask amiss and God cannot grant my petition, at least not yet. Sometimes there is more that I must do for them in addition to my prayers. Sometimes I need to pray with tears, even as Jesus wept.

Sometimes my own faith needs strengthening. In every circumstance, however, I know that His will is always the perfect plea.

77

Equal Rights

For ye are all the children of God by faith in Christ Jesus. For as many of you as have been baptized into Christ have put on Christ. There is neither Jew nor Greek, there is neither bond nor free, there is neither male nor female: for ye are all one in Christ Jesus.

Galatians 3:26-28

The above verses are often quoted by Christians concerned with women's rights and involved in the feminist movement. And it is true, as God has declared, we are all one and we are all equally important as members of the body of Christ. But these verses do not say that we all have the same responsibilities in our service for God. They do not imply that we can set aside the God-given roles that men and women have been assigned, both in the Lord's church and in our own families. We need to recognize that God has much to say regarding this subject in both the Old and New Testaments.

The Word of God forthrightly declares that the man should be the head of the family. After Adam and Eve sinned, God explained the roles that each must assume for their own sakes:

> Unto the woman he said, I will greatly multiply thy sorrow and thy conception; in sorrow [pain] thou shalt bring forth children; and thy desire shall be to thy husband, and he shall rule over thee. And unto Adam he said, Because thou hast harkened unto the voice of thy wife, and hast eaten of the tree, of which I commanded thee, saying, Thou shalt not eat of it: cursed is the ground for thy sake; in sorrow [toil] shalt thou eat of it all the days of thy life.
>
> Genesis 3:16, 17

Men, therefore, are intended to be the head of the family and must toil to provide for it. Women are primarily responsible to not only bring forth children but to care for both them and their husbands in the home. These were traditional roles throughout the Old Testament. God chose men to be heads of the tribes of Israel, to be priests in the tabernacle and the temple, to lead His people in peace and in war, to be His oracles and scribes, and to rule as kings in Israel until the King of Kings should come.

Those nations who served other gods were often ruled over and seduced by evil women and priestesses in their pagan temples. These nations God eventually destroyed. Israel, on the other hand, when in favor with God, maintained the traditional male and female roles that God had given them.

When godly men were in charge, the nation flourished. Joshua said, "but as for me and my house, we will serve the Lord" (Joshua 24:15).

And when godly women served their families, the home was blessed.

> Who can find a virtuous woman? for her price is far above rubies. The heart of her husband doth safely trust in her. She looketh well to the ways of her household, and eateth not the bread of idleness. Her children arise up, and call her blessed; her husband also, and he praiseth her.
> Proverbs 31:10, 11, 27, 28

The woman described above was also a businesswoman. She bought a field and planted a vineyard. She also made fine linen and sold it. The significant point regarding her demeanor is that her family came first. Her husband may have been the head of the home, but she was the heart of the home. I think God wants women to be the homemakers. God had said, "It is not good that the man should be alone; I will make him an help meet for him" (Genesis 2:18).

And brethren, nothing has changed in the New Testament. I think it is significant that Christ chose twelve men to be His apostles. I think it is significant that the apostles appointed men to be the deacons and elders in the early church. Clearly, God has given men the primary responsibility to govern in the Lord's church, to glorify Him in all that they do, and, especially, to lead their families in paths of righteous living. God will hold men accountable for these duties at the judgment seat of Christ.

For a man indeed ought not to cover his head, forasmuch as he is the image and glory of God: but the woman is the glory of the man. For the man is not of the woman; but the woman of the man. Neither was the man created for the woman; but the woman for the man.

1 Corinthians 11:7-9

Wives, submit yourselves unto your own husbands, as unto the Lord. For the husband is the head of the wife, even as Christ is the head of the church: and he is the saviour of the body. Therefore as the church is subject unto Christ, so let the wives be to their own husbands in every thing. Husbands, love your wives, even as Christ also loved the church, and gave himself for it.

Ephesians 5:22-25

Let your women keep silence in the churches: for it is not permitted unto them to speak; but they are commanded to be under obedience, as also saith the law. And if they will learn any thing, let them ask their husbands at home: for it is a shame for women to speak in the church.

1 Corinthians 14:34, 35

I believe this simply means that women were not meant to be pastors or leaders in the local church. It does not mean that they cannot serve as help meets, and certainly God intends them to witness for Him before their family and friends. The influence of virtuous women in the church and in the home can accomplish as much or more than all the words of their male counterparts.

Instead of demanding their equal rights in positions of leadership, I think women should look more circumspectly to the unique role and special talents that God has already given them. Only women serving the Lord humbly in their own special way can make the church, their homes, their neighborhoods, and yes, even the nation in which they dwell a sweet-smelling savor unto God and a joy to their families.

78

Carnal Christians

For we know that the law is spiritual: but I am carnal [fleshly], sold under [possessed by] sin.

Romans 7:14

Some well-meaning Christian author has coined the sentence, "If He is not Lord of all (our time, talents and possessions), He is not Lord at all." This opinion parallels a similar thought of total commitment and consecration expressed in the popular hymn, "I Surrender All." Neither is honest or true, and they are causing many bewildered new Christians to doubt their own salvation.

When we are born again into the family of God, we begin as babes in Christ and God expects us to grow into mature Christians. But throughout our earthly lives, we are carnal to some extent, because we are yet in the flesh. We have fleshly appetites that need to be restricted and gradually overcome.

The Apostle Paul wrote to the new Christians at Corinth:

And I, brethren, could not speak unto you as unto spiritual, but as unto carnal, even as unto babes in Christ. I have fed you with milk, and not with meat: for hitherto ye were not able to bear it, neither yet now are ye able. For ye are yet carnal.

1 Corinthians 3:1-3

The Apostle Peter instructs new Christians, "As newborn babes, desire the sincere milk of the word, that ye may grow thereby" (1 Peter 2:2).

We should understand that when we are first saved, we are not miraculously and immediately made the fully spiritual person that God wants us to become. We are immediately indwelt by God's Holy Spirit; He becomes our new conscience; the Holy Word of God becomes our spiritual food; and we begin to grow spiritually. We do not all grow at the same rate. Sometimes we resist the Spirit and neglect our study of the Word, and there is little growth. Some foolish Christians remain inordinately carnal and babes in Christ for most of their earthly lives.

All our works will be tried at the judgment seat of Christ, and the carnal Christian will suffer loss. "Every man's work [deeds and witness] shall be made manifest... and the fire shall try every man's work of what sort it is.... If any man's work shall be burned, he shall suffer loss: but he himself shall be saved" (1 Corinthians 3:13,15).

The carnal Christian will be ashamed at the coming of our Lord, and the Lord will be ashamed of him. But by the matchless grace of God, the truly born again believer will still be saved. He will be restored spiritually, even as the Apostle Peter after his vehement denial of even knowing the Lord. You and I may doubt whether the carnal Christian was ever saved at all, but the Lord knows those who are His. He will hear their confession, acknowledge their repentance, and forgive them. I believe there will be a lot of tears at the judgment seat of Christ. Even those who receive a reward will acknowledge their shameful carnality and shortcomings when they stand before God! "So then every one of us shall give account of himself to God" (Romans 14:12).

The real danger of carnality is the possibility that those who are yet carnal may not be saved at all! The carnal may be deceiving themselves. "But be ye doers of the word, and not hearers only, deceiving your own selves" (James 1:22).

"Not every one that saith unto me, Lord, Lord, shall enter into the kingdom of heaven; but he that doeth the will of my Father" (Matthew 7:21-23).

We are commanded not to judge one another, but we need to be concerned whether or not many of our professing brethren are really saved. As we have stated in previous articles, an intellectual assent to the reality of Jesus Christ and the practice of calling Him "Lord" is not enough. Church attendance is not enough, and faith without works is dead (*see*James 2:26). We will find that our carnal weaknesses are no excuse at the judgment seat of Christ.

Therefore we are admonished to "work out your own salvation with fear and trembling" (Philippians 2:12). We need to know that Satan is a terrible adversary and the Great Deceiver! *His most hopeless captives are those who think they are saved but have done nothing about it!*

"Wherefore . . . brethren, give diligence to make your calling and election sure" (2 Peter 1:10).

Our carnality should remind us of our need for spiritual growth. For if there is no growth, there is evidently no life and we are still dead in trespasses and sin. Most professing Christians have in childlike faith confessed Christ as Savior. Most have been baptized and have joined a church. However, only the truly born again are aware of the Holy Spirit now dwelling within them and are concerned regarding their need to know and do His will. Only the genuine babe in Christ is hungry for the written Word. Only the converted sinner wants to separate himself from the shallow activities of this world and spend more time in prayer and fellowship with his brethren in Christ.

Few of us have really surrendered all. However, we should have learned that the peace which passeth all understanding, the joy of the Lord, and the wonderful fullness of life which God has promised come only as we recognize that we are growing spiritually, that we are appropriating the likeness of Jesus even while we are yet in sinful flesh, and that living for His glory is our most important priority!

Soon we shall leave behind our carnality and He will clothe us with new and perfect bodies which will never know the ravages of sin. We shall be like Him forever.

79
Christianity Is Common Sense

There is a way which seemeth right unto a man, but the end thereof are the ways of death.

Proverbs 14:12

We find all human souls inclined
To make the goal of life
Comprise a present peace of mind,
A future free of strife.
We grasp at every joy along
The way we choose to go;
We seek like all among the throng
More happiness to know.

There are but two roads, only two,
And man may walk but one.
Life's sorrows, both will lead us through,
We find escape for none.
Neither leads us as we plan,
Though hopefully we trod;
One is called "the way of man,"
And one "the Way of God."

All men who plan "the way of man"
Their road of life to be,
Have sought since ever time began
That perfect destiny.
In islands far from tyrants' reign
In treasure of the mine,
In science, seek they peace to gain;
In might, they still decline.

In social planning now they seek
The world to educate,
That freedom of a man to speak
Will banish fear and hate.
But no such plans can ever win,
For man must first be freed
From all the evil lusts of sin,
From selfishness and greed.

If happiness were only found
In earthly wealth control,
Then from the theories they propound,
We might attain the goal.
But happiness cannot be bought,
Nor peace the world acclaim,
For earthly treasures fade and rot
In earth, from whence they came.

The pleasures of the world provide
No balm in time of sorrow,
And joy, where fleshly lusts abide,
Is lost upon the 'morrow.
"The way of man" denies belief
In future life with God,
And hopes with death, to find relief
From grief, beneath the sod.

A Christian goes the other way,
As God would have us go,
A way prepared since light of day
First shown on man below.
A way of love, a holy love
Above all humankind,
As space beyond the stars above
Transcends the human mind.

For God in mercy sent His Son
To die, that we might live;
To guide us 'till the victory's won,
Our errors to forgive,

To teach us love and bring us peace,
Despite the cross we bear,
To give us joy and His release
From every earthly care.

Oh, God's way is a happy way,
Secure, whate'er befall,
And when the Christian kneels to pray,
God listens to his call.
He gives us power to attend
His Word, and work His will,
He gives us grace that knows no end,
Life's meaning to fulfill.

A Christian is the wealthy heir
Of treasures stored on high.
For God has promised mansions there
No earthly wealth can buy.
A Christian's life is diligent,
And joy beyond compare
Is found in little efforts spent
For those whose lives we share.

"Suppose there is no God, what then?"
The unbeliever cries,
"Suppose there is no life again,
When once a person dies?"
Then weigh the evidence at hand
Which life was most complete,
Which life attained the goal as planned,
Which ended in defeat?

"If I am wrong, I've naught to lose,"
The Christian can reply,
"My life is still the way I'd choose,
For both of us must die.
And just suppose, as well you might,
That Christ should come again,
Suppose you're wrong, and I am right,
What then, my friend, what then?"

80
Quotes to Remember Me By

God gave you two ears and only one mouth for a reason.

There are none so deaf as those who won't hear.

A Christian can't *go* to church; he *is* the church wherever he goes.

If you're so smart you don't need to attend a Bible class, you ought to be teaching one.

You can't be a secret Christian.

The one who knows that he knows nothing compared to what there is to know, knows the most.

There are really only two kinds of people in the world: lost sinners and saved sinners.

Religion is one of Satan's favorite weapons.

We were saved to serve.

Are we standing on the promises or just sitting on the premises?

Sex is God's wedding present.

The Holy Bible is the only infallible source of truth and knowledge in the world today.

If more of our theologians would spend less time reading one another's books and more time prayerfully studying the whole Word of God, there would be less division among them.

As Christians we are called to live and work and witness *for Jesus' sake.*

We need to feed on the "meat of God's Word" to know and proclaim *God's answers to the mystery of life.*

A Christian should *never* do anything just because everyone else is doing it.

A Christian should *seldom* do anything just because he wants to.

A Christian should *always* do anything that he knows would be pleasing to God.

"And *whatsoever* ye do, do it heartily, as to the Lord, and not unto men. Knowing that of the Lord ye shall receive the reward of the inheritance: for ye serve the Lord Christ" (Colossians 3:23, 24, italics added).

About the Author

Albert Charles McCann was born October 25, 1919, in Highland Park, Michigan. He knew poverty, loneliness, and tragedy while only a child. He lost his father at age nine. His mother experienced several severe heart attacks and became a complete invalid when he was only thirteen. Al sold newspapers and did odd jobs to pay the bills.

He wrote a letter to Henry Ford and asked for admittance to the Ford Trade School. His letter was channeled down to the proper sympathetic authorities, and he was accepted. He started work at fifteen cents per hour. Ford Motor Company took a liking to the boy, and when he graduated at seventeen, they kept him in the drafting room of the school for an extra year and encouraged him to change his major from toolmaking to engineering, paying for the necessary college courses. He worked days and studied into the wee hours of the morning for many years.

A very wise pastor led him to the Lord when he was seventeen and put him to work in the local church as a youth leader and Sunday school teacher. He has been teaching and counseling ever since—for over fifty years, except for a stint in the army.

He retired from Ford as Manager of Plant Engineering, Cleveland Engine Plants, in 1975, and since then has started condensing some of the thousands of Bible lesson he has written into short articles that are compellingly different than most Christian books in the market today. Al tells it like it is, for he has lived it.

He and his wife, Marge, now reside in Fort Myers, Florida. They attend the Christian and Missionary Alliance Church in Shell Point Village. The Lord has blessed them with two married sons and six grandchildren.